Discovering, Developing and Expanding the Real You

I0099079

By Darren T. Carter

Foundation Publications
www.FoundationPub.org

Discovering, Developing and Expanding the Real You

Discovering, Developing and Expanding the Real You

Start To Finish is a powerful and practical book, which calls followers of Jesus to release their faith and God-endowed gifts toward the agenda of the Kingdom of God in the earth. Unlike many books today, in this volume you will be moved beyond theory and theology into implementation and application especially in the area of Biblical entrepreneurship. Use this book for personal development and for mentoring others.

Jim Hodges ~ President
Federation of Churches and Ministers International

Darren's latest book *Start To Finish* does something rare in today's Christian literature. In practical teaching followed by clear examples he helps the reader apply mission. I believe in mission since I see it as the heart of the gospel. Application is the missing ingredient in most books today, however it is the very wisdom you will discover in this book that will help you fulfill your mission.

Artie Davis
Pastor, church multiplier and author of the book "Craveable"
Executive director of The Sticks Network and Conferences

Darren Carter writes from real life experience in *Start To Finish*. His teachings are like plant food for growing a fruitful, good life. Lessons gleaned from him and his friends and peers guarantee success to the faithful student. Mark these pages with a highlighter. Get ready for a bigger understanding of who God wants you to be. Be willing to be stretched to size.

Pastor Robert Summers
Mountain Creek Community Church & World Prayer Center in Dallas, TX

Darren Carter has created a powerful book to help you find that unique place God has for you. *Start to Finish* can be a useful tool for you individually, your small group, your church family, your business or charity group. Darren puts it best when he says, "One can have the best product, service solution or message, but basic principles must still be applied in order to achieve the intended objective. Creating a plan of action and purposefully implementing that plan is essential for a project to reach its full potential."

Dr. Dale Roach
Director of Missions, Moriah Baptist Association and Like A Team

Discovering, Developing and Expanding the Real You

As a coach, one of the first steps to helping others move forward is discovery, awareness and an understanding of where they are at this very moment in life. *Start To Finish* is like a coaching manual to success in life. It will take you toward understanding the freedom that God has given you in being authentically and magnificently you, and then takes you through the process of realizing how important personal leadership is in living the intentionally abundant life for which you have been born. Read this book prayerfully and reflectively. You will see a Holy Spirit shift take place and your life will be changed forever.

Robert Ricciardelli,
Life Coach and Director of Converging Zone

Occasionally someone moves past the burning initial revelation and like the two men on the road to Emmaus constrain Jesus to stay with them and sup with them. Darren in *Start To Finish* has done that with these truths. He has assimilated in breaking the bread of Life, which has allowed him to bring us this written articulation, not a how to do book, but how to Be. It's only out of this place of true Rest that we can serve correctly.

Steve Chase
Director Connecticut River Media Ministries

Do you want to know your life purpose? Are you a business professional, student or church minister? Darren's inclusion of personal biographies helps the process to become reachable. As a missionary in East Africa I found myself inside of these wisdom biographies. This book has keys to make us more passionate and effective in our endeavors. Read *Start To Finish* and get ignited again in the special purpose God has for you. We need more honest voices like the ones in this book who share with inspiration and humility.

John Michael, Missionary and Co-Founder of Shiloh House Mission in Kenya, Africa

Darren's book is proven and is guided by Paul's words in Eph 4:15-16 (NIV). 15 Instead, speaking the truth in love, we will in all things grow up into him who is the Head, that is, Christ. 16 From him the whole body, joined and held together by every supporting ligament, grows and builds itself up in love, as each part does its work. *Start To Finish* is a must read.

Jeff Pelletier, MA, Host, Speaker and Consultant
"God's Work in Progress

Discovering, Developing and Expanding the Real You

Discovering, Developing and Expanding the Real You

INTRODUCTION

Start to Finish is the third book in a three volume series called *Foundations for Life*. The series corresponds with the *Building Your Spiritual House* workbook. The third section of the workbook is, *Kingdom Ministry Through The Church*, which focuses on discovering and using your gifts. In conjunction with that section the purpose of this book is to make sure we are established in a foundational understanding of the gifts we have each been given and how to apply them to our daily lives.

The series, *Foundations for Life*, does not have to be read in order, but it will greatly benefit you to read *Running the Race to Win* and *Worship In An Age Of Excess*. I am building on previous teachings, and it is beneficial, although not necessary, to read the books in sequence. It will also be helpful for you to use the workbook *Building Your Spiritual House* as an additional study supplement. (Get the first section for free along with my free online school of discipleship at: www.FoundationPub.org.)

The goal of this book is to lay Biblical foundations concerning the discovery of your gifts, the development of them and the practical implementation of those gifts. It is truth that is simple, attainable and applicable. It is my goal to present truth in such a way that you are moved beyond intellectual assent to application, which transforms your character and manner of life.

THE GOSPEL IN ALL SPHERES OF LIFE

The gospel is intended to affect all aspects of our life and even society. It is the responsibility of each member of the body of Christ to use their gifts wherever the Lord places them. It is the breaking down of false ideas that separate the clergy from the laity, the sacred from the secular.

If you have a teaching gift, it does not necessarily mean you are to serve in a traditional church way; you may teach in a school or university. You could use your gift as a motivational teacher to business leaders. We are called to impact this world, and we are the church no matter where we have been called to serve.

A missional movement applies the gospel to all spheres of life. It is nothing new, but large segments of the body of Christ are finally awakening to the fact that we are a multifaceted body serving in various arenas. [1]"Our job as Christians is not to take over the various communities in our world; it is however, to penetrate them, to be present, to provide God's alternative to evil, to demonstrate Christ's relevance there, to be as good a representative as possible for Him and His church."

KINGDOM ENTREPRENEURS

An entrepreneur is an individual who organizes, manages, and takes on the risks of an enterprise. Everyone possesses certain abilities which can be developed, utilized, shared, and expanded. While we may not fit the traditional definition of entrepreneurs, it is beneficial to adopt a similar mindset. In Matthew 25:14-30, Jesus taught this exact same principal. In this parable He taught us that we are each to be kingdom entrepreneurs taking the necessary risk in developing and expanding our influence. We may not be like Steve Jobs or Mary Kay, but we can still have a lasting impact on our family, community, and city.

To be a kingdom entrepreneur is the same thing as being a committed disciple. Everyone needs to be a disciple and be involved in making disciples since we have been commissioned to do so. Whatever He has taught us we are to teach others. This not only applies to biblical knowledge, but it goes over into all areas of life.

I remember growing up in a small Texas town during the 1970's and having a working mother. She was an example of someone who affected the community in which she lived. She and

Discovering, Developing and Expanding the Real You

a friend stepped up to the plate and became Boy Scout leaders in a male dominated culture. They also affected that culture by bringing African American poor children into that organization. She was not well liked by the power structure of that town, but she had an impact on the lives of those children. Many went on to be college graduates due to those two ladies' influence. The essence of a kingdom entrepreneur is impacting the lives within your sphere of influence.

Christianity is more than knowledge; it's about living life. The best way for you to teach someone how to run a business or ministry is to let him or her work with you for a season. We must educate, but we must also apply education with hands-on experience. On-the-job training is the best instructor. We need to train people in all fields of life to follow Christ and be a witness for Him in their field of ministry. Impacting society requires people to stand up and make a difference. Everyone in the church must be willing to make disciples.

The audience I am trying to reach is disciples who have the attitude of an entrepreneur and want to do their part in changing the world around them. You may be a homeschool mother, businessman, church planter or local politician trying to change your community. I am going to lay out seven traits in this book that will help you develop the expanding attitude of a kingdom entrepreneur in your life. It does not matter what place in society in which you are called to serve, these traits will help you to fulfill the purpose of God for your life.

PURSUING THE PURPOSE OF GOD

The goal of this book is to take you on a journey as an individual and show you how your journey is intricately tied together with others to fulfill your purpose. You can never fulfill the will of God solitarily; your purpose will ultimately be fulfilled in conjunction with others.

We hear many people, even non-Christians, talk about life as a

Discovering, Developing and Expanding the Real You

journey. The issue I want to discuss that separates the believer from the non-believer is the "will of God" or fulfilling the purpose of God for your life. It is a journey birthed, led and matured by the active work of the Spirit in our lives.

Once we discover our calling and the potential we possess, we must move along a journey of faith to fulfill our purpose. We each go through stages along this journey. In Romans 12:2, Paul talks about the will of God being good, acceptable and perfect. These are not three separate directions we can choose but are *levels of growth* in the one will of God. John the apostle talks about these three levels of growth as children, young men and fathers (I John 2:12-14). Jesus uses the analogy of the growth of grain by saying "the ear, the blade, and full head of grain" (Mark 4:28). In the one will of God, we must grow through these three different levels to fulfill our full potential.

Let's take a look at the three levels of growth as we press on to fulfill our particular calling. The first stage is what John calls children, which is the dependent stage. This is the place where we discover our calling, potential and ability. At this stage, we are *dependent* on others. This is where we are nurtured and encouraged by others and where we begin to study and discover our gifts; however, we are only in a place of training.

The second stage of growth is what John calls the "young men" stage, which is a stage of independence. This is the place of stepping out and exercising, or using, our abilities. At this stage, we begin to realize we can do what God has called us to do. We take hold of God's ability and begin to bless others with it. No longer are we waiting for someone to tell us what to do because we know the will of God and how to release our God-given ability.

The third stage is where we become fathers and mothers, which is the stage of interdependence. This is the place where our gifting begins to mature into a level of not only using our abilities but also working with and helping others fulfill their callings. At this stage, we become mature enough to see that we don't have everything it takes to get the job done. We learn to combine our potential and abilities with others to create something greater together.

KINGDOM SUCCESS

It is important to define success from a biblical perspective. I define success as discovering, developing and expanding in the will of God for your life. It is the Father's heart that we expand the kingdom of God, and our lives are the vehicle through which that expansion is achieved. To effectively do this, we must have a practical application of truth in our lives. It is necessary to move from planning to action in order to achieve our goals.

Here's a thought to ponder: Can you envision a life that moves beyond a quest to acquire "stuff" toward a dream that defines how you can contribute more to the lives of others? In practical terms, what would that look like? Most of us want to make a lasting mark on the world, leaving it a better place than we inherited. Perhaps your new dream can encompass how you can optimally apply the discovery of who you are and how to use and expand your gifts toward a better tomorrow. It doesn't need to be a large program; just be yourself in fulfilling your objectives. The aim in this book is to present timeless principles that can be applied to everyday life.

My objective is to teach effectively so that you acquire both knowledge and practical application of that knowledge. I do not claim to have all the answers, but I aim to make the content relevant to your daily lives and activities. The principles discussed can be applied in various contexts and may not be implemented the same way everywhere, but they will be workable. If you put the truths presented in this book into practice, you will discover, develop, and expand your skills and abilities.

Note: In this book I use the word *kingdom* quite often. The word *kingdom* can mean many different things to different people depending on what you have been taught. I want to encourage you to read what I have written on this subject in my book *Building Your Spiritual House: Introduction Section III,* which you can get on Amazon.

I also address the subject of the *kingdom* in fuller detail in my second book of this series *Worship In An Age Of Excess.* It is important for you to understand how I use the terminology of the kingdom, so you don't misinterpret what I am writing. I am encouraging you to read my ideas, so you don't read your own ideas or what others have taught you into what I am saying and therefore miss the perspective I am presenting.

Discovering, Developing and Expanding the Real You

Chapter 1

DISCOVERY: The Key To Success

"The kingdom of heaven is like a treasure hidden in the field,
which a man found and hid; and from joy over it he goes and sells
all that he has, and buys that field."

~ Matthew 13:44 ~

I think everyone wants to have success in life; it is
something intrinsic to human nature. Yes, everyone wants
success, but doesn't everyone succeed? I do think success
depends on how you define the word, so let's not look at this
"success thing" from the world's point of view. I have already
defined success in the introduction of this book as discovering,
developing and expanding in the will of God for your life.
It is from this reference point that I am starting and finishing,
since this is the viewpoint of the kingdom.

If you want to succeed, you must be willing to do whatever
it takes to get to your goal. Jesus used two analogies to make this
same point when He said before we go to war or before we start to
build, we must first sit down and count the cost (Luke 14:28).

I have one purpose and that is to make disciples, and I am
going to look at success in the context of discipleship. You should
read the gospels once again and as you do, contemplate what Jesus
had to say about discipleship. If you have not already done so,
you may want to read my first book *Running The Race To Win – A
Radical Call To Discipleship* it is a practical guide to the
practices required for all disciples.

Discovering, Developing and Expanding the Real You

If you think you are going to fulfill God's purpose for your life and it is not going to cost you, then this book will challenge your ideas. I am not suggesting the implementation of self-made plans, which is commonly encouraged by most success books. I am advocating that you learn how to submit to a kingdom dream for your life. If you don't start off on the right foundation, everything else will be null and void. We must start right if we want to finish; therefore, we must build for long-term success. To build for the long term, you must take the time to dig deep.

Kingdom thinking is being willing to strip everything down to the bare basics then build according to the ways of God. John the Baptist, who was a preparer of the way, did not tell us to build on the faulty foundations of self-desire. He told us to rip up the old by the roots, if necessary and burn it with fire. If you ask me, that is radical terminology! He emphasized that for long-term success, it's essential to focus on genuine substance rather than superficial hype that fades under pressure. We aim to build on enduring principles that remain stable while following God's will.

Let's look at the word *radical,* since I have also discussed it in my other writings. The word *radical* comes from the Latin word *radix*, which means root. So, to be radical is to get down to the root of things, penetrating its essence and not being distracted by the many sidetracks. The root of discovering, developing and expanding the real you is to look inside yourself and dig deep to remove any barriers in your life that are keeping you from your true self. Isn't this what Jesus taught concerning the kingdom of God? In all the parables and pictures that Jesus used to describe the kingdom, He taught this idea of radical commitment.

YOU HAVE TO DIG DEEP TO FIND THE REAL YOU

Self-discovery is probably one of the greatest challenges we have in life. What am I called to do? What is my purpose? What are my gifts? I think these are basic questions that each of us ask from time to time in searching for purpose in this life. At the same time, it is what most people are missing in their lives; they simply

Discovering, Developing and Expanding the Real You

wander through life with no purpose.

If you look at most people who attend college, 44 percent change their majors between the second semester and graduation. At the same time a high percentage that do graduate seldom work in their field of study. George Barna has done studies indicating that only a small percentage of believers, around 20 percent, have identified their gifting's and consistently sought to use them in a practical way.

When it comes to gifts, it seems that many in the church are confused and the reasons abound--traditional church roles, misunderstanding of scripture or humanistic philosophies. Under the Old Covenant, we see three main roles: prophet, priest and king. In the New Covenant, there are three main "gift sets".

I want to help you see gifts from a biblical viewpoint. The first gift set I want to briefly look at is in Ephesians 4:11, which speaks of the gift of Christ. Five gifts are listed here--apostle, prophet, evangelist, shepherd and teacher. If you want more information on each of these gifts, see Appendix A in the back of this book. Each of us is to operate in these five dimensions because of being imparted to and impacted by them. If you would like more in-depth understanding on this subject a great book addressing this is *The Permanent Revolution* by Alan Hirsch and Tim Cathchim.

The second gift set is found in I Corinthians 12:1-11. I use the word *gift*, but the word *gift* is actually not in the original language. The Greek word used for "spiritual gifts" in verse one is *phanerosis*, which means to "make visible" or "to display" the Spirit. The word of wisdom, word of knowledge, gift of faith, gifts of healing, working of miracles, prophecy, discerning of spirits, tongues and interpretation of tongues are manifestations of the one Spirit of God. Every believer can operate in one of these manifestations at the Spirit's direction.

Due to certain people's gift mix, they tend to operate more consistently in certain manifestations of the Spirit. It does not mean the manifestations of the Spirit are not available to everyone; it just means that due to calling, commitment and gift mixes, certain individuals will see greater consistency in the visible operation of the Spirit. To get more information on these manifestations, go to Appendix B at the back of this book.

The third gift set is found in Romans 12:6-8. A few teachers call these "gifts of grace," but I am going to refer to them as "motivational gifts". The gift set listed in this portion of scripture is prophecy, service, teaching, exhortation, giving, managing and mercy. To get more information on these motivational gifts, refer to Appendix C.

IT REALLY IS A FREE GIFT

I like to say that Ephesians 4:11 is about *function* while Romans 12 is about *motivation*. We need both function and motivation; while realizing it all depends on grace to develop our abilities and expand our influence. However, one of those paradoxes in the kingdom is that we must dig deep to receive a free gift.

Grace and all it implies is a free gift, but you have to be willing to yield your whole heart to its power for it to motivate you. Start to finish; it is all about grace. All we are doing is learning to recognize, develop and expand the grace gifts freely given to us.

Grace is one of those words most Christians use, but I find few really understand all it entails. (To get greater details on this subject of grace, read Chapter 4 *Running The Race To Win* www.FoundationPub.org.) Paul said, "I am what I am, and His grace toward me did not prove vain; but I labored even more than all of them, yet not I, but the grace of God with me" (I Corinthians 15:10). Paul understood that his motivation to fulfill the will of God and work hard at it was due to the free gifts he had been given.

Our vision, hard work and persistence have to be grounded in the free grace of God or we just labor in vain. Dead works is what we do when we pursue the will of God outside of the grace of God. When all is said and done, the only thing that matters is completing the will of God, which is our success, and

Discovering, Developing and Expanding the Real You

there is plenty of grace available for each of us to complete His will.

I have had to dig deep at several junctions or turning points during my journey to discover the grace of God in my life. I am not going to give you some quick formula that is going to help you discover the grace of God and the gifts that come along with it, since in my experience, it just does not happen that way. Life is a journey where we continually learn to open the free gift of grace and yield to His power in our lives during each season through which we walk.

At the age of 19, I was in my first semester of college, and I was delivered from addiction. During my first few months of experiencing the grace of God, I knew that His hand was upon my life to be a minister of the gospel, but I also knew there was a grace upon my life for business. In that time period, very few people could put the two graces together. I soon discovered that I had a combination of gifts like all of us have. Let's look at what I first discovered about myself during this period of time.

In my second semester of college, I had to take a literature class and was required to do a lot of writing. One day, my professor for this class called me into her office. As I sat there, she began to tell me I had a real gift for writing. I knew that I liked expressing my thoughts through the written language, but I did not realize it was actually an artistic way to express a teaching grace upon my life.

What my professor saw in seed form has now become a tree from which others can eat and grow. The fruit of which you are now partaking took years of growing, pruning, sinking my roots down deep through tough times and just simply learning through reading others' viewpoints.

I operate as one of my primary functions in the Ephesians 4:11 gift of teacher. It is a gift that has been freely given to me, but I've had to dig deep to see that gift mature to the place where it profited others and me. Once you discover your gift, it will take time, hard work and perseverance to see your gift mature. If

Discovering, Developing and Expanding the Real You

someone tells you otherwise, they are either a false prophet, trying
to sell you something or leading you down the path of short-term
success and long-term failure. What I am saying is there are no
easy paths but the path you are to follow.

ONLY FREE PEOPLE CAN BE THEMSELVES

Have you ever been to the zoo and watched the caged animals?
If so, you can see that even though these animals have been
rescued from death, they are still not free to be themselves. It is
said that injured lions mostly die not from their injuries but from
the pain of being unable to do what they do best. We are much
like the lion in that respect. We have been set free so that we can
truly become the person we were created to be and when we are
not that person, we die inside. Proverbs 13:12 say's hope deferred
makes the heartsick. Could this be one of the main reasons we see
so much mental illness today, because people are jailed in sin and
a total lack of purpose?

"Are you free?" is the question you have to ask yourself. If
you are free, you are going to be comfortable in your own skin.
Paul said, "I am who I am." Paul understood his gifts. He
developed them and expanded them because he was free. His
freedom allowed him to reach his potential. In Romans 12, Paul
helps us identify the differing motivations each of us has been
given; he then tells us not to compare ourselves with each other (II
Cor. 10:12).

If you are trying to emulate someone else, you are not free.
You can learn from others, but you are unique. It is your
uniqueness that makes you who you are. You must not focus on
yourself but look to the grace that sets you free. Grace is about
taking the mundane and ordinary and transforming it into the
special and extraordinary. Grace does not focus on our
insufficiency but on the all-sufficiency of the cross and the
freedom of being found in Him.

It was William Shakespeare who said, "God has given you one
face, and you make yourself another?" You may not realize it, but

Discovering, Developing and Expanding the Real You

not being yourself is actually a subtle form of hypocrisy. I have a
great desire to see the church break out of the box. We should be
the most unique, creative people on the face of the earth. I don't
think people hide from their true uniqueness on purpose, but we
have been bound so long it is hard to break free. Let's look at
three main areas that bind people from being free. Many times, we
become like the prisoner who has been so institutionalized that he
can't imagine living free. Let's look at these three main areas:

- **Traditionalism**: Jesus talked about allowing traditions to keep us
  from the will of God.
- **High Mindedness**: Paul said that when we think more of
  ourselves than we should, we miss our true calling. We have to
  accurately assess our gifts, abilities, strengths and weaknesses.
- **Limited Thinking**: When we limit our thinking, we keep
  ourselves bound to the ideas that have shaped our thinking and
  kept us from His purpose.

DON'T LIVE IN BOXES

The most frustrating thing in life is trying to be someone you
are not. We cannot live in the boxes that society or religion makes
for us. We cannot live in the boxes others make for us regardless
of their good or bad intentions. When we think of peer pressure,
we normally think of insecure teenagers giving in to the wrong
advice of peers. The reality of peer pressure is that it does not just
apply to teenagers. All of us can be affected by the pressure to
live in the boxes of groupthink.

Groupthink is a psychological term used to describe something
that happens in the human population; we call it the "herd
mentality" in the animal kingdom. The results of giving into
groupthink are the loss of creativity, entrepreneurial attributes,
healthy dialogue and an outward look to expansion. George Patton
said, "If everyone is thinking alike, then somebody isn't
thinking." Every healthy business, family, church or organization

gives room for diverse gifting, dialogue, and thinking.

I find it interesting to look at the context of Romans 12 where Paul lists the different motivational gifts. If you look at verses one and two of this chapter, Paul is addressing the boxes that hold us back from utilizing our gifts. Some of these boxes are our sinful nature, ethnic groups, religious groups, political groups, pop culture and etc. It is thinking that is in opposition to the word of God. We have to be willing to challenge our thinking and the thinking that we encounter in our environment if we want to lay hold of our purpose.

At the age of 21, I attended a church that had a discipleship school. I learned many good things in the two and a half years that I attended this fellowship, but I also saw much damage done to people's lives due to groupthink dominating their thinking. If you were willing to think outside of the parameters of this group, you were quickly labeled, isolated and bullied until you got back into the box or left the group. I find many religious groups, businesses/political parties, operate by these principles and it leads to their demise. They eventually lose what they worked so hard to protect because they do not allow people to have the liberty to be themselves.

I have found that people have the tendency to put you in the box of their strengths. For example, people with a gift of service will serve tirelessly, but if they are not careful, they will judge others for not having the same passion for service that they have. Have you ever been around a missionary that wants to make everyone a missionary and if you don't succumb, you are somehow not spiritual?

You will always have a problem when you impose your motivation on others, as each person has their own passion that motivates them personally. When you impose your passion on others instead of helping them discover their own motivations, you are actually working against the freedom of grace in their lives. Grace works alongside helping others to encourage them toward freedom and the full utilization of their abilities.

Groupthink imposes its ideas on you, bringing you into

submission to the group regardless of your individual gifts. True freedom is discovering yourself then freely using your gifts to serve others. If you are not free, you will never be yourself and your growth will be stunted.

True success comes from simply coming to terms with whom you are and pursuing your passion. You have to be comfortable in your own skin because if you are not, there are plenty of people that will try to cover you with theirs.

Saul tried to put his armor on David, but David, at a young age, knew who he was and refused it, which caused him years of trouble. But when all is said and done, you have to be you. You are going to have years of trouble either being yourself or trying to be someone else. Save yourself some time and be yourself!

STAY WITHIN YOUR BOUNDARIES

Paul used a principle that I call our "measure of rule." We don't live in boxes, but we are limited to our measure of rule or boundaries. In the physical world, a boundary is a property line. It defines where you end and someone else begins or where you end and something else begins.

Paul, whom I could safely call the most effective apostle in New Testament times, realized that he was not called to do everything. He could not be everywhere or change the whole world by himself. Although we each have a specific calling and vision, it is limited to the measure of rule God has distributed to us and the boundaries of our gifting.

Paul, in speaking of his apostolic ministry, says, "We shall not boast extravagantly but rather stay within the limit of the sphere which God has allotted to us" (II Corinthians 10:13 New Berkley Version). Paul understood that God had given him a specific vision for ministry and specific places to impact.

We need to see our measure of rule in regard to both *visionary calling* and *boundaries*. This can be clearly seen in Paul's life. Paul tells us that his distinct visionary calling was to minister to the Gentiles. In Acts 28, when Paul was speaking of his heavenly vision, he says that Jesus specifically told him he was being sent to preach to the Gentiles.

Paul further clarified this in Galatians 2:7-9 when Paul, referring to his visit with the elders of the church in Jerusalem, says, ". . . seeing that I had been entrusted with the gospel to the uncircumcised (Gentiles), just as Peter had been to the circumcised (Jews) (for He who effectually worked for Peter in his apostleship to the circumcised effectually worked for me also to the Gentiles), and **RECOGNIZING THE GRACE THAT HAD BEEN GIVEN TO ME** . . . gave to me and Barnabas the right hand of fellowship that we might go to the Gentiles, and they to the circumcised (Jews)." (Emphasis mine.)

Paul was defining his calling and restricting it to what God called him to do within the grace of God upon his life. It does not mean that Paul did not do anything else, because he did. We know that he went first to Jewish synagogues or gathering places anytime he entered a new place to expand the gospel. We also know that he put up a thorough defense of the gospel to the Jewish authorities in Jerusalem.

Paul stayed within the boundaries of his Gentile calling when it came to the big picture and kept his priorities straight. If you are an accountant, you may be great at managing numbers, but that does not mean you can manage people well. It is possible that you have a skill for both and as you discover your strengths and weaknesses, it will help define your boundaries.

We don't want to be too rigid with boundaries, but they are very helpful in enabling us to accomplish our purpose in this life. Boundaries keep us from the distractions of all the lesser pulls that take us away from the main thing, since they keep us in our sweet spot. When you hit the golf ball in the sweet spot the ball stays in bounds but miss that spot and you could waste some time looking for that little ball. Let's look at several things that boundaries do for us:

• Boundaries help us to *define responsibility.*

- Boundaries help us to *define accountability.*
- Boundaries help us *focus our energy.*
- Boundaries help us *reject distractions.*
- Boundaries help us *see our part and do it.*

FEARLESS TO BE YOURSELF

Aristotle said, "To avoid criticism say nothing, do nothing, be nothing." It seems that many people settle for this way of living in mediocrity instead of pursuing purpose. The book of Proverbs calls this type of thinking a snare, which is a trap for catching animals. If you are afraid of failure or man's criticism, do nothing, because if you do something, you will experience both.

When we allow the opinion of others to become a motivating factor in our lives, we become captivated by their ways instead of the word of God. One of the main reasons listed in Romans 12:1-2 for having our minds renewed is so we can walk in the will of God, which takes time and grows in stages. If we are confused due to outside influences, we need to allow the word of God to dig deep into our hearts. Confusion causes paralysis and double mindedness, which makes us unstable and unable to accomplish anything.

We each have a primary motivational gift, although this does not mean we don't have any other motivational gifts or any other gifts for that matter. I have a primary motivational gift of manager, but that does not mean I don't serve or give it just means I am primarily motivated to manage and lead. I also have a primary gift of teaching which I use in writing, communicating both in ministry and business.

In ending, I want to share five simple principles, which apply to your life concerning your gifts:

1. **Discover your gifts**: To know your calling is to have purpose and know the direction you are going. The will of God is what matters in life, and once we have a glimpse into that, we can live life with

purpose

2. **Cultivate your gifts**: To cultivate your calling, you will have to carefully remove the influences and people who seek to choke your calling. Stay in an environment that is going to cause you to grow and not die (Mark 4:18-19).

3. **Guard your gifts**: Paul told Timothy to guard his God given potential (II Tim. 1:14). Satan is constantly trying to use a multitude of circumstances, attitudes, things, and people to devour your calling. You must be diligent to protect the gifts and calling of God on your life.

4. **Share your gifts**: Your calling is given for the benefit of others and not you only. When we share our gifts, it not only blesses others but it increases our ability. We grow by exercising our gifts.

5. **Limit your gifts**: You cannot do everything. You only have the potential to fulfill your particular calling. Be content to labor in the grace that you have been given.

Chapter 2

LEADERSHIP: The Key To Starting Right

"The kingdom of heaven suffers violence and violent men
take it by force."

~ Matthew 11:12 ~

Who could count the numbers of books written on the subject
of leadership? While many books have been written about
leadership, it remains for many a misunderstood and elusive
quality. The capacity for leadership exists in everyone, but most
people never take the time to develop it. Leadership is
determination, courage, confidence, making the right choices and
the ability to get results.

The key to leadership is first of all about self-government; as
such, the above scripture is very pertinent. The text in Matthew
11:12 could be translated as, "the kingdom of heaven is forcibly
entered, and violent men seize it for themselves." If you want to
live the kingdom life, you have to seize it with all of your heart; it
does not just come to you. (To get more details, study Lesson 38
in *Building Your Spiritual House* at www.foundationpub.org)

The essence of self-government is personal responsibility. It is
making the right decisions motivated from the kingdom of God
within your heart. It is demonstrated by your willingness to accept
responsibility for your own behavior--what you think, say and do.
You can achieve your goals by yielding to the authority of the
kingdom, not by following others' directives. It is something He
has made available, but you have to take hold of it with all of your

heart--like Caleb in the book of Joshua, who at 80 years old took hold of his inheritance. You must have that same type of tenacious attitude that will not allow anything to stand in your way.

If you want to lay hold of your purpose, you must take both hands and seize it for yourself. It is a free gift we have to intentionally possess; no one else can do it for us. For this reason, we each have to develop leadership qualities to lay hold of our full potential. I am not saying that we are all gifted with positions of leadership in the church, business, and politics or any other number of visible leadership positions. The qualities I want to share with you are applicable to everyone and will help you develop the leader within you, whether or not it is in your family, school, church, city or business.

VISION AND A PERSONAL MISSION STATEMENT

Vision cannot be taught, but it must be caught. What I am saying is that you can get a parrot to repeat your vision; however, when vision is in a person's heart, you can't stop that person. We must do more than memorize our mission statement, but we must embrace it with our actions. Our vision should be clear, concise, and easy to understand. Once we identify our strengths, we must present them clearly. Just like cleaning fish after catching them, writing a business plan involves defining your vision and mission.

A business plan is a strategic map showing how to fulfill the endeavor you are undertaking. On an individual level, it is called developing a personal mission statement. It has been said that he who fails to plan, plans to fail; therefore, to clarify your vision, you should write down and clearly articulate who you are, where you want to go and how you plan to get there.

You fill many roles. To stay balanced, you need to address each area of your life: **family, finances, professional, physical** (exercise and eating), **social and spiritual**. It is important to address the whole person, because if you focus on only one area and neglect the other, the ride will get bumpy. Like a wheel, your

Discovering, Developing and Expanding the Real You

life runs smoothly when you give appropriate attention to each area.

Take some time right now to go to Appendix 1 where I have added a place for you to write a personal mission statement for each of these six areas. Use a pencil so you can write several drafts, as you will more than likely review, update and change them ever so often. Circumstances change and we can't be so rigid that we are not adaptable, but at the same time, we don't want to be tossed with every wind. "Determined flexibility" is the way I like to look at writing a personal mission statement. It is not the Ten Commandments but simply a guide to help us stay on course.

The mission statement should be broad enough to govern every area of your life but specific enough to reflect your uniqueness and gifts. Habakkuk 2:2-3 instructs us "to write the vision clear so that he who reads may run". The goal of writing a mission statement is to help give you directions and to stay on track. Jesus only did that which the Father directed Him to do and did not waste time being distracted. Paul said he was obedient to the heavenly vision. If you want to accomplish your purpose, you need to clarify, write down, communicate and remind yourself of your purpose. We easily drift; therefore, we need to remind ourselves where we are headed.

GOOD MANAGEMENT IS TEAM BUILDING

If you don't know your strengths, you won't know how to build a team or fulfill your part on a team. Since God has limited us to a certain measure of rule in our vision and calling, we mustlearn how to flow with others. This makes teamwork an utter necessity.

Let's look at this in the context of a family. Husbands and wives are each going to have their unique personalities and strengths. The problem with this is that our uniqueness usually turns into opportunities for strife; however, we should try to turn them into opportunities for cooperation. Diversity is the way of the kingdom, but it is a diversity that works in unity.

If you look at the bible in the context of the home, I agree that the husband is to be the head or leader, but the wife is to be the manager. Look at Proverbs 31 and you will see the mark of management. I don't want to put any couple in some type of predetermined box.

As a couple, my wife and I use the principle of teamwork in our marriage. The highest order of marriage is not submission and authority but actually the principle of *one flesh* where teamwork is lived out. Each couple must work out their own salvation in their marriages with fear and trembling, which the bible gives you room to do. Don't allow some religious straitjacket to impose views that are impossible or impractical for you. The home is the building block of any ministry, business, school, etc. and if you don't get it right there, you won't get it right anywhere else.

Team building is, of necessity, to fulfill your purpose, as no man is an island to himself. Entire books have been written on the subject of team building and it is here that I just want to make a few points. We must understand the difference between **leadership** and **management**. It is important for you to make this distinction because the gifts that you possess will determine which role you are to play.

In the book, "Leadership, Management and The Five Essentials for Success," the author instructs us that it takes both leadership and management. We just need to be humble enough to do our part. True humility is bowing the knee to the part that you are to play, not trying to be someone you are not.

[2]"To properly understand leadership, we must first distinguish it from management. Confusing management with leadership has caused many an enterprise to fall short of its potential, and in many cases, to fail altogether…Both leadership and management are required for the administration of almost every venture, but they must be recognized as separate and kept within their own spheres of authority." To make it simple, leaders are big picture oriented while managers are detail oriented, and you need both to

Discovering, Developing and Expanding the Real You

be successful.

Stephen R. Covey says that "management is efficiency in climbing the ladder of success; leadership determines whether the ladder is leaning against the right wall." Leadership sets the course we are to follow while management helps in practically applying the vision. The two must learn to cooperate to accomplish anything of value. Many times, you will find much tension between these two aspects of accomplishing a task. It is by communicating clearly that we are able to get the most out of each other's parts.

Teamwork consists of everyone having the heart of a servant and realizing we each have our own perspective but working towards the same goal (To get more details on the subject of serving read Lesson 40: The Call To Serve at www.foundationpub.org) Leaders cannot be so overpowering that they do not give their implementers room to work out the details. Managers often need to step back and look at the big picture or they will get so caught up in the details that they miss the purpose of what they are doing.

God has composed His body so that it demands teamwork. Biblically speaking, *teamwork is not an option, but the only way for effective vision to be implemented and accomplished.* If you look at any successful church, business, ministry, community or family, a common ingredient is teamwork.

In looking at biblical examples, it is easy to see that God has always worked through teams: Moses and Aaron, Joshua and Caleb, Jesus and his apostles, Paul and Barnabas, and Paul and Timothy. In addition, we have the husband-and-wife team of Aquilla and Priscilla. The list could go on. Jesus gathered a core team who were joined to Him and to one another. In fact, this was one of His highest priorities. This also became a priority with the apostles He sent out, and it is still a priority for those who want to build according to kingdom principles.

Discovering, Developing and Expanding the Real You

THE NEED FOR ORGANIZATIONAL STRUCTURE

Organization is almost a dirty word among some groups. However, it takes some level of organization to accomplish just about any task. A body without an organized skeletal system is just a mass of tissues, organs and is useless and unable to accomplish anything without the structure that the skeletal system provides.

It is not my intention to write a book about developing organizations. It *is* my intention to demonstrate that to develop and expand the real you, you must learn to work with organized teams, whether in a ministry, a business or an educational setting. A team without organization is chaos.

Organization is not the end but a means to the end, which is helping others. When Jesus fed the five thousand, he organized them into groups (John 6). The apostles set up an organized program to feed and take care of the widows in Jerusalem (Acts 6). Paul, responding to the prophetic word that Agubus gave concerning famine in Judea (Acts 11), organized the collection, gathering, and distribution of needed supplies to that region (read the book of II Corinthians describing this effort.)

Organizational development is inseparably related to fulfilling needs, whether we are getting a product to market, educating a child or feeding the hungry. Structure should be designed to meet clear objectives and sometimes, once those objectives have been met, may be discarded.

To keep organizational structure for structure's sake is legalism. Jesus talked about new wineskins that must be flexible (Luke 5:36-38). We live in a fast-paced, moving world and we need to keep up to date by changing with the needs presented to us.

Organization is needed, but organization is not sacred. What I mean by that is never let how an organization works become your focus. I have found there are many ways to get from point A to point B, so let's not get caught up in the method. We do, however, need a method or organizational structure to get the task fulfilled.

Discovering, Developing and Expanding the Real You

SELF-DISCIPLINE: THE KEY TO STAYING ON TRACK

When I mention the word discipline, I am not using it in the context of correction but consistency. It is like a runner who uses self-discipline to get out and train every day. We have plenty of reasons to quit what we are doing, but it is only through consistent day in and day out hard work that we achieve success.

Paul said that he labored abundantly due to the grace of God upon his life. He was not sluggish about the promises and purposes of God but diligent to do his part. We are partners with God and partnership means we have a part to play. We can't just sit back thinking something is going to happen and that God is going to do it. No, He has commissioned us to join with Him. He's not going to write the book, build the new computer or hand out the food--we are His hands and feet. (To get more details on partnership read Lesson 39: The Yoke Of The King at www.foundationpub.org.)

It was said that through faith and patience, Abraham inherited the promises of God (Hebrews 6:12). The Greek word for patience in this context means *consistent*. Abraham stayed with it consistently. Ask someone how they accomplished something, and they will tell you they stayed with it.

Watch a golf game. The reason golfers make the game look easy is because they have consistently spent 8-10 hours a day practicing. Playing an instrument seems effortless for musicians, but countless hours of practice go unseen. Self-discipline is the key to success; it is the rails, which keep us on the track. Self-discipline stays with it no matter what anyone else is doing or who is watching. It is laboring in the grace of God for the audience of the One to whom we all must give account.

DIVERSIFY YOUR SKILLS

It may seem like a contradiction when I say we need to

diversify. Yes, we need to focus on and develop our gifts, but we must be flexible when it comes to how we make an income. We all need finances to survive in this world. Paul did not always make his living through preaching the gospel. He diversified when it came to earning an income.

I have seen more than once a person's source of income dry up. If you do not diversify your skills, you could be left struggling to survive. In this fast-moving world, we cannot depend on the same source of income throughout our lives. It used to be that a person would get a job and have it for the next 30 years. Now it is estimated that people change jobs every 3-5 years.

I have had to learn how to diversify my skills to provide and care for my family. As a single person, it is much easier to live, travel and care for yourself. It is for this reason that Paul said single people can more easily serve the Lord and give themselves to Him in single-hearted devotion (I Cor. 7:33-35).

I want to take a few minutes and address those who feel called to what we call "a preaching ministry." Paul did say that those who preach the word have the right to also live from their preaching (I Cor. 9:7). He used the analogy of a farmer eating from his own crops or a shepherd partaking of his own animals. Paul had this right and did take advantage of it, but at times, he chose to set an example of laborious work. At other times the provision was just not available from the people to whom he had been sent to minister, so he had to diversify his skills and do what it took to accomplish the will of God.

I have ministered in a full-time setting and lived off the earnings from my preaching, but I also had to learn how to use the skills God gave me to earn a living in other venues. I have worked for small companies and Fortune 500 companies. There are seasons to our life, and we must understand every season so we can cooperate with the plans of God. I can tell you that I have not always understood His leading, but He knows why He leads the way He does.

Discovering, Developing and Expanding the Real You

CONTINUING EDUCATION

To fulfill your purpose, you must be willing to continually learn and sharpen your skills. To be a leader, it is important to be a reader. Reading is considered a fundamental discipline for leadership. What are you reading today that will make you a better person tomorrow? It is estimated that successful people read one to two books per week. Often, they read multiple books at once. To grow, you must read. The Greek word for disciple is *mathetes* and simply means a disciplined learner.

As I previously stated, I was saved in my first semester of college. I finished my associate's degree and went to a discipleship school for two and a half years. Soon, I was on the mission field. Within a few more years, I was pastoring a church, and while there, I completed my bachelor's and master's degrees in theology. I went back on the mission field for a few years and then came back to the United States. Like many others whom I have met with ministry experience and a degree in Theology, I found myself out of place in the real world. I had to decide to pursue a typical ministry or redefine myself. Well, since I don't like boxes, I chose the latter.

At the age of 33, I went back to school and finished my bachelor's degree in business management. I was willing to continue my education and stretch myself in areas outside my comfort zone. The experience I have gained and the broadening of my views because of being in the business world could not have been duplicated in a traditional ministerial setting. Not only has it been a great experience, but also, I have been able to use the practical concepts I learned and apply them to ministry situations.

I used continuing education to diversify my skills, and it paid off economically. If you find yourself in a similar place, take advantage of it. The company for whom I worked paid 80% of my education costs; it was a win-win for us both. I can say my degree helped me grow, learn and obtain new opportunities.

We have to be willing to learn and I mean continually learn, until the day we die. If we are not learning, we are falling behind and missing all God has intended for us. I want to encourage you to find a book about your passion and read it.

COMMUNICATION: LEARN TO EXPRESS YOURSELF

I don't think I can overemphasize the importance of communication. We all need to learn to communicate better, and we must continually work on honing both verbal and written communication skills. Let's look at this on the micro scale of the family. Paul uses the family as a prototype of learning how to lead. He sets this standard: If we cannot lead our families, we should not be given responsibility to lead in any other context, since we will simply reproduce the same results (I Tim. 3:5).

I have seen that communication problems can normally be traced back to the family. A breakdown in communication results in divorce, as well as many unhealthy patterns in the lives of children and then we wonder why we have so many problems with school and workplace violence.

Communication is a key to effective leadership in any endeavor you undertake. It is important to work on your verbal and written communication skills. If you do this, it will not only help you professionally but will be of personal benefit to both you and your family. How we communicate reveals much about who we are and our maturity level. The better we are at conveying our message clearly, passionately and with loving care, the more success we will have.

Jesus was a good communicator. He always understood the audience to whom He was speaking. To communicate effectively, you must develop your message for the audience you are addressing. Jesus spoke to the 5,000, 70, 12 and 3. He had a message for each situation. You must understand your audience. Great communicators don't tell people what they want to hear but what they need to hear by crafting their message in such a way to help people improve their lives.

It is a proven statistic that the greatest fear people have is a fear of public speaking. Leaders must learn to develop the skill of public speaking. Fear and self-consciousness will keep us from fulfilling the will of God. It is important that we yield to the power of the Holy Spirit who will help us do all that we are called to do. It is true that some are going to do more public speaking than others and some will be better at it than others. In Appendix 2 at the back of the book, I provide some simple ways and resources to help you develop both your speaking and writing skills.

A BASIC UNDERSTANDING OF ECONOMICS

Jesus talked a lot about money, and most times, it was in the context of discipleship. He also used it in reference to ministry support, taxes and miracles. To neglect a basic understanding of money is to refuse to listen to the words of Christ. Any endeavor you undertake in this life, from raising a family to running a business or ministry, requires a basic understanding of economics.

I am not talking about being a math whiz but knowing enough to manage, at a minimum, your household budget. Credit card companies will give an 18-year-old a credit card even though the same person most likely will not understand the difference between a 5% or 18% interest rate. Neglecting a basic understanding of how our economic system works is a lack of wisdom.

I find it amazing that we teach kids how to do algebra, but many times, these same kids can't balance their bank accounts. For example, I once worked with an engineer who had a master's degree in engineering, but his motorcycles were being repossessed due to mismanagement of his personal finances. Stewardship is a basic discipleship principle. Jesus went so far as to say that if you don't know how to take care of money, you wouldn't know how to take care of the spiritual principles of the kingdom of God.

You may find yourself in debt by making bad decisions or you just got caught in an economic storm being laid off from work.

We can't despair if we find ourselves in debt, but we do need to get out a shovel and start digging. What I mean is we need to be consistently wise with our money. You can find many resources to help you. One good resource is Dave Ramsey (daveramsey.com), who has made teaching others about getting out of debt into a career.

As I previously said, not everyone has to be an economic whiz, but it would be wise to learn how to handle money or have someone involved with your life that knows how to handle money. If you run a small business and don't know how to keep your books, spend the extra money to have a bookkeeper. As I have discussed, my wife is good with numbers and enjoys doing budgets. Since she is the one with the gift and motivation, she performs the task with the grace of God.

DON'T LET THE TIME GET AWAY FROM YOU

You only have 24 hours per day, 7 days per week and 365 days per year. You cannot create time, but you can either waste your time or take advantage of your time. Time is your most valuable resource. Aristotle Onassis, a wealthy businessman, once said, "I have learned the value and importance of time; therefore, I work two additional hours each day and in that way I gain the equivalent of one additional month each year."

The secret to time management is learning how to use your time wisely. Solomon told us to look at the ant:
Take a lesson from the ants, you lazy fellow. Learn from their ways and be wise! For though they have no king to make them work, yet they labor hard all summer, gathering food for the winter. But you – all you do is sleep. When will you wake up? 'Let me sleep a little longer!' Sure, just a little more! And as you sleep, poverty creeps upon you like a robber and destroys you; want attacks you in full armor (Proverbs 6:6-11, LB).

We must be aware of time thieves that try to steal our time. Your time thief may be television, sports, the Internet or just a lack of organization. Wasting time does not just happen, but it is

Discovering, Developing and Expanding the Real You

something that we actively allow to happen. A habit develops over time and usually becomes an unconscious act. It is important that we address these bad habits that have been stealing our time and develop healthy habits, which will help us, as Paul said, buy back time (Eph. 5:15).

It does not matter if you are a homemaker, minister, student or businessman; you must learn to manage your time. The struggle most of us have with time is keeping a schedule. I want to emphasize the importance of prioritization. Putting first things first is the key to effective time management; that way, we are doing what we are supposed to be doing instead of just keeping to a schedule. Robots can be programmed to keep a schedule, but they cannot fulfill the purpose of God. Jesus is our pattern, and He had one purpose, which was to fulfill the will of the Father. We must organize our time in such a way that it enables us to more fully walk out the purpose of God in our lives.

I tend to be more of a big picture person, so I don't really like making lists and schedules. To accomplish our purpose, we need to define our goals and priorities, as we can waste a lot of time not knowing where we are going. Lists and checklists help to solve these problems. [3]"Making purposeful lists and checklists is an 'art', a skill to be developed and perfected. If used properly, this skill has the ability to radically impact the efficiency of almost anyone. Like any other 'art', there are basics to be learned that apply to almost everyone, but after that you must develop your own style."

In Appendix 1 at the back of this book is a guide that will help you make lists and checklists. Use this tool, along with your vision and goals, to prioritize your list and accomplish your purpose.

Chapter 3

Fellowship: The Key To Development

"Truly, truly, I say to you unless you eat the flesh of the Son of Man and drink His blood, you have no life in yourselves."

~ John 6:53 ~

Jesus made an interesting series of statements in Matthew chapter 7:13-23. In this section of scripture, He is specifically dealing with the true verses the false. He then boils it down to something very simple in verse 23 by saying, "I will declare to them, 'I never knew you; DEPART FROM ME, you who PRACTICE LAWLESSNESS'" (emphasis mine).

That is pretty heavy if you sit back and think about it for a moment. We could spend our days working for God and doing things without ever having an intimate relationship with Him. What I am attempting to do for you in this chapter is to help you be grounded in intimate fellowship first with our Father then with one another, since it is the only pathway to true kingdom development.

Intimacy is the pathway by which we attain advancement in the kingdom of God. You may advance in this world in a number of ways, but it is not the foundation of the kingdom. True lasting purpose is established in intimacy and advancement comes out of that foundational relationship.

Discovering, Developing and Expanding the Real You

It is through the gospel of John that we glimpse into the heart of the Father found in the ministry of Christ. John uses many word pictures to describe the intimate relationship that our Father wants us to have with Him. We are pictured as sheep that intimately know His voice (John 10:27). The gospel of John gives us a visible picture of the intimacy Christ had with His disciples, calling them His friends (John 15:15). They ate together, served together, laughed together, prayed together, and worshipped together. John himself reclined his head upon Christ's chest at one point during the Last Supper (John 13:23).

In John chapter 14, we see the role of the Spirit in teaching, guiding, empowering and living in us. In John chapter 15, we then see the correlation between obedient abiding in Him and the power of spiritual growth produced by that life. It is expansion by abiding. It is then in John chapter 17 that we see the highest order of intimacy and that is oneness.

Have you ever been around a couple that have been married for many years and have worked in a covenant relationship? If you have then you have witnessed their oneness. A couple of this maturity will display oneness that cannot be accomplished any other way but through long-term intimacy.

In the same way, we are to be intertwined with the nature of Christ so that we are not working for Him but simply manifesting the nature within us. Our lives simply become an overflow of our relationship with Him. If we build on any other foundation one day we will find ourselves working for something other than the kingdom of God. Our primary purpose must be intimacy and everything else is simply the overflow of divine love.

Practicing lawlessness is a result of pursuing purpose without intimacy. It is trying to fulfill our calling in our own way and using our gifts with selfish ambition. We are doing the work, but we have forgotten the Lord over the work. Desiring to succeed is an ambition we should have; however, it is not for ambition's sake alone, but it is to accomplish the will of the Father. When the focus of our lives is to be in an intimate relationship with our Father, we will find our motives and desires coming into alignment with His will.

Simple obedience will be our hearts desire. Intimacy will allow you to:

- Align to the purpose of God.
- Keep your motives pure.
- Work for the right reasons.
- Have the proper type of ambition and motivation.

RELATIONSHIPS ARE THE AVENUE FOR DEVELOPMENT

It's no secret that other people influence our lives. This is a widely understood fact of life. Sciences have been created to study how people affect one another. Sociology and psychology are studies of human interaction. Advertising, marketing and economics have a firm foundation in understanding the influences that we exert on one another. This isn't a recent phenomenon. Ancient proverbs speak of men sharpening each other as iron sharpens iron (Prov. 27:17).

I have never been in a relationship that has not been strained at some time. All relationships will be strained, but it is how we come out on the other side that determines our development. We can't control the way others are going to react, but we can learn to react in the character of godliness.

I can tell you from experience that God will allow you to be in difficult relationships to stretch you, challenge you and rub you the wrong way because He is working something out of your life that could not be worked out any other way. Look at David's life and the relationships he had. His brothers despised him, his first mentor turned on him and his first wife scorned him.

Change would be the operative word to describe what relationships do for us. We are going to be changed because of relationships whether good or bad. Think back to the first job that you had. I worked part-time for a hospital part-time while I was in high school. I had to learn to work with women, doctors and office workers. The duties I had to fulfill were to pick up the dirty linen and then clean offices at the end of the day. I learned at an early age how to maneuver through these different personalities and stay on task to complete my duties. It was my interaction with all of these different types of people that prepared me to do well at my next job.

Reflect on the relationship you have with your wife or husband and if you are not married, then a close friend. Think about how you have changed as a result of the relationship. The change we go through in relationships is a result of fellowship.

The Greek word *Koinōnia* is translated as fellowship and means: "Participation in anything, the using of a thing in common." When I think of the word *Koinōnia,* I think of the word partnership. A partner shares, loves and works together. When you do this, you are going to change because you will rub off on one another.

The Bible is full of relationships and development. Jesus and the twelve, Paul and Timothy are clear examples of mentoring relationships. I like the term coined by Steven Covey when he describes Win-Win relationships. Ideally when seeking out a mentoring relationship, we want to seek out relationships that are going to be beneficial to both parties.

To be honed you have to bring a skill to the table that is beneficial. For example, if someone is a chef, then he has no interest in mentoring an accountant interested in banking. It would not be a Win-Win situation since the skills and passions don't match. If you are simply giving spiritual mentoring, then having similar skill sets is not necessary since the relationship will be one of merely spiritual empowerment and support.

Skills and character are honed by the acceptance of constructive criticism. I don't know anyone who likes to be corrected; however, iron-sharpening-iron is a direct reference to this activity. I will use myself as an example. When writing a book, I will do my best to send it out to other writers so that they can give me constructive feedback. I don't always like the feedback that I get, but looking through a different set of eyes helps me challenge what I think and helps me get it right.

I want to encourage you to seek out those with whom you can have a Win-Win relationship regarding developing your gifts. One word of warning that I will give is don't become too exclusive in this approach. I have found that many times God will have you learn from someone and once you have what you need, he will move you on to your next learning session.

It does not mean that you must break up a relationship but that your next relationship will build upon what has already been imparted. Don't let people play the exclusive game with you, especially in the church. We have two permanent covenants in the New Testament, marriage and Christ. Everything else is subject to change.

We don't always need a close working relationship with someone for him or her to be our role model. In today's electronic age, we can glean from others in so many different ways. It is helpful to watch creativity at work in other people and get ideas to help us. Find people who are doing things right and model them. You don't have to copy them but let them inspire you and gain from their experience.

WE ADVANCE THROUGH SERVING

It is an oxymoron that we advance in the kingdom by serving. Honestly, I have always struggled in this area because of the seeming contradictions I have found in scripture. We are supposed to make of ourselves no reputation while at the same time, we are to be seekers of our purpose and are to expand our gifts. I have found the way to bring together these two opposite approaches is to merge them into one. We should always have the attitude of helping others even while we are fulfilling our purpose. We can serve our way to the top because in the kingdom, the bottom is the top.

Let me use myself as an example. If you sign up for my e-newsletter at my blog page www.FoundationPub.org then I will send you a free copy of the first section of my book *Building Your Spiritual House*. I spent hours and hours writing, correcting and printing my first book. Why would I give it away for free? It is simple. I want to serve you and help you succeed in your faith.

I have one passion and that is to see disciples made. I am successful when you mature in your faith and if my first book is an asset to you, then you are more than likely going to want to buy some of my other books. You may even want to buy a hard copy of my free book and make disciples of others in small groups, a discipleship class or Bible School. I advance my purpose by serving you free material.

I love this Mexican food restaurant in Brownwood, TX. On Sunday's they serve a buffet. It is good food and throughout the meal, servers will walk around the restaurant handing out freshly grilled steaks, shrimp and chicken. The serving attitude that goes above and beyond what you are looking for is what makes you want to come back. The good food you pay for is what you expect, but when you are served beyond what you expect, then that venture is sure to expand.

A good church will excel at giving out more than it takes in. Have you ever been to a church where you feel like you are there to serve them? I have been in plenty of those churches, and it is repulsive and eventually brings decrease not expansion. People know when you truly care about them or if you are just out to get something from them. If you want to be successful in the long-term, then serve others. It will lead to your expansion whether it is a business, ministry, friendship, etc.

HUMILITY: THE FRUIT OF AUTHENTICITY

It is credited that Abraham Lincoln once said, "You can fool some of the people all of the time, and all of the people some of the time, but you cannot fool all of the people all of the time." What do you think when I mention the names Enron, Ernie Madoff or Tiger Woods? It is not transparent and authentic, is it? Once you have ruined a name, it is hard to clean it off and once

Discovering, Developing and Expanding the Real You

you have tarnished a brand, it is hard to get back buyers. It takes work to create a good name and a selling brand, but it is very easy to damage.

Humility is a trait I don't think many of us understand today. I am not talking about self-humiliation or false humility since they are just non-authentic and really nothing more than pride. True humility is both transparent and authentic because it is simply about being who you are in the hands of God.

Moses is a good example of true humility. He was obedient to leave everything behind and suffered the ridicule of that decision. It was on the backside of the desert that Moses came to terms with himself, and the burning bush was the turning point. It was testified about Moses that he was willing to endure affliction with the people of God than the passing pleasures of sin.

Moses surrendered to the call of God and was willing to do whatever it took to get himself into the place of purpose. However, the burning bush was the commissioning and filling of that surrendered heart. If you don't have your burning bush experience before you become a leader, then you will follow the fate of so many other fake and fallen leaders.

The fire of God that produces holiness, transparency and authenticity, which are the traits that will keep you kneeling in humility when the winds of trials come your way. If you don't build on the foundation of humility, then you will eventually crack under the pressure of keeping it all together in your own strength. Humility realizes that without the grace of God, then nothing stands.

The pathway of humility is a pathway of brokenness. I am not speaking of destruction but of a heart that has been humbled, surrendered and dedicated to the Father. Just after the upper room of fellowship with His disciples, Jesus went to the Garden of Gethsemane to pray. It was here where He completely surrendered to the will of the Father.

It is interesting to note that this is the same night in which Jesus partook of His last Passover with His disciples. Just as they

Discovering, Developing and Expanding the Real You

finished Passover and right before they entered the Garden, there arose a heated discussion about who was the greatest among them.

On the night of the Passover, Jesus gave a clear discourse on the difference between selfish ambition and laying down our lives to serve. It is not the self-serving who are great in the kingdom, but it is those who pour out their lives to serve others.

James describes the one who has selfish ambition as someone who has given him or herself over to demonic wisdom (James 3:13-16). When we are driven by demonic wisdom, it will always result in jealousy and strife. However, the wisdom flowing down from the Holy Spirit will bring unity of heart. This will produce an overflow of peace and the ability to work as a team member to create something you could not create on your own.

People often start their journey of faith focused on themselves, but growth involves looking beyond oneself. In Mark 10:45 Jesus set the example for us to follow because, **"the Son of man came not to be ministered unto, but to minister, and to give his life a ransom for many"**. We have to learn to live our lives as He did, not to be ministered unto, but to minister, to pour out. This is just what we find Jesus doing in the Garden - pouring out His life for others. Service must be the foundation of whatever we are building since it is the cruciform life of faith.

PARTNERING THE POWER OF SYNERGY

Synergy is defined as two or more things functioning together to produce a result that is not independently obtainable. It really does define the true power of fellowship, which we have already established as being the power of partnering.

The focus of synergy is God's miraculous power at work. Jesus was God, but He could not fulfill His mission alone He needed partners. It was said of the original man that it was not

Discovering, Developing and Expanding the Real You

good for him to be alone. Loneliness is a curse of modern society since man was created for fellowship with God and one another. Studies have shown that cancer patients who had no friends around them were more likely to die than those who were surrounded by friends and others who cared.

A story that exemplifies the power of synergy happened in the summer of 1904 at the St. Louis World's Fair. It was a hot day and ice cream vendor Arnold Fornachou ran out of paper bowls because his ice cream was so popular. He was losing customers. In the booth next to him was a pastry chef named Ernest Hamwi from Syria, Damascus.

Ernest was selling a thin pastry that no one was buying when suddenly he was struck with an idea. He took one of his warm pastries, twisted it into a cone shape and rolled it in sugar. He took the invention to Arnold the ice cream vendor who was looking for bowls and had him put his ice cream on top of the cone. The customers loved the ice cream on top of the cone and history was made with the creation of the first ice cream cone. This was accomplished by the power of synergy.

In looking at the purpose of God for our lives, synergy occurs when our lives encounter others to create something we could never create alone. It is the power of community being awakened, which is what the church is supposed to be 'a city set on a hill'. Let me give you a brief testimony of what happened in our family. Our son is academically oriented and had a hard time fitting into the school he was attending. Although he did not like sports he had to go to P.E. It came out that he was being bullied for two years during P.E. classes. God was faithful to make a way for us and with the power of synergy, we have been able to educate our son in a way that alone we could have never done alone.

The couple God brought us together with had degrees in both chemistry and physics. Our son was taught math, science, history and English by this other family. I taught him sociology and the Bible. It was the power of synergy producing something we could not have done through our own family. Fellowship is the power of synergy and how your gifts will be developed according to the purpose of God.

The church is about learning how to live in a community. We should be working with each other and training the younger members, whether in age or faith, to develop their gifting's. We need to train people in all fields of life to follow Christ so they can be a witness for Him in their field of ministry.

Chapter 4

Creativity: The Key To Constant Renewal

"No one puts new wine into old wineskins; otherwise the wine will burst the skins, and the wine is lost and the skins as well; but one puts new wine into fresh wineskins."

~ Mark 2:22 ~

If you want to accomplish something of value, you have to be willing to go beyond where you have gone before. The world is full of people who have settled for the comfortable status quo of existence instead of pursuing their purpose. If you are willing to press on to something new, it will take breaking outside the familiar with fresh new ideas.

You can settle for mediocrity, or you can press beyond what is familiar to you and be willing to face the unfamiliar. It will be a challenge and will more than likely cost you, but to remain fresh in your faith, family and career, you have to be willing to have your life turned upside down from time to time.

Jesus talked about new and old wineskins. Author Richard Florida polled 20,000 creative professionals and gave them a choice of thirty-eight factors that motivated them to do their best. The top two factors were challenges and flexibility. Let's look at this in reference to new and old wineskins. If we want to succeed

Discovering, Developing and Expanding the Real You

by accomplishing the will of God, we have to be willing to be challenged and remain flexible.

The wineskins Jesus talked about were made out of freshly killed goats or lambs and the whole animal was actually used. You had to use skins from freshly killed animals so it could stretch during the wine fermentation process. If you have ever gone through a time of change, you know that you were both challenged and stretched beyond what you had known before. It is actually a process of death and new life.

One thing we can learn from this analogy that Jesus used is that new life will require sacrifice. No one likes sacrifice, but if you want to experience the new, many times there are things you have to leave behind which will most likely require you to sacrifice something you valued in the former season.

What do you think the horseshoe maker thought when the train was invented? He did not immediately see a loss in business, but if he had foresight, he would have challenged himself to learn a new trade or at least make sure his son was prepared. The horse was not done away with, but as a mode of transportation, it was killed and replaced with a new, more reliable technology.

We are constantly going through this process of change. Take a look at recent times. If you work for a newspaper, you can choose to hold on to that old wineskin or stir up your creativity to move into something new. Those who are willing to take the challenge to learn something new and remain flexible will have the new creative wine poured into their hearts. The reality of the times we live in is that if you don't rise to the challenge and remain flexible, it can threaten your survival.

CHANGE IS NOT OPTIONAL

We are going to change whether we like it or not since we live in a world that is constantly on the move. The world around us is changing at breakneck speed on a daily basis. We have to be adaptable to our environment while remaining true to ourselves. We can choose creativity, which helps us to reinvent ourselves, so

Discovering, Developing and Expanding the Real You

that we can succeed in the will of God.

John Wimber was a man who was willing to challenge the status quo and be flexible to what the Spirit was doing in his day. He was willing to take chances and step out of the ordinary way of doing things to create something new. John was the founder of what is now known as "The Vineyard Movement." He was instrumental in bringing change to the "Evangelical Church" in America and spurred the renewal movement worldwide. He stood out as one who was willing to challenge the way things have always been and be flexible enough to move with those changes.

In the book *Creation of the Media,* the author Paul Starr relates a funny (at least from an American viewpoint) but tragic story. [5]"After taking power in 1917, the new Soviet rulers could have invested in telephone networks, as other nations were doing at that time, but chose instead to emphasize another emerging communication technology--loudspeakers."

It is hard to imagine, but true, that the Soviet Union had no foreword thought. They failed to see the changes that were rapidly happening around them. The Soviets were blinded by a command-and-control system. [2]"The czarist mentality of the previous century still prevailed. The Soviets focused on technology that reflected imperial values: higher-ups telling the common people what to do."

Creativity is prophetic at heart. What do I mean? To be prophetic is to challenge the status quo and remain flexible enough to continue to change. Freedom is at the heart of prophetic creativity. Every church, business, family and industry is going to become stale from time to time. Prophetic creativity is the fuel that keeps us in a state of renewal to see where we are headed, and it is always changing to meet the next challenge.

New ideas don't flow from the top down in some sort of holy funnel, but the Spirit is poured out on all flesh (Acts 2:17). The wisdom you need to make the next big decision does not have to come from the CEO, but it might just be an idea from the guy out on the factory floor. Wise companies have learned to listen to their employees. This applies to families, churches and your small businesses. We were created for freedom. To desire freedom is something intrinsic to the human soul. It is only the truly free who can create to their fullest potential, as they are merely reflecting the ultimate Creator.

[6]"Einstein, one of the greatest paradigm shifters of all time, reminds us of our sacred duty to dream God's dreams and rediscover the transforming power of the imagination." Jesus was also a big believer in the human imagination. [6]"Jesus teaches that how and what we imagine is truly serious and profoundly spiritual. If we allow our imaginations to be caught up in the kinds of things Jesus taught and the kinds of miracles Jesus performed, we will be ready to live like Him – according to the will of the Father and in the power of the Spirit."

PRAYER RELEASES OUR CREATIVE IMAGINATION

Godly imagination that is grounded in the gospel and inspired by the Holy Spirit is hopeful, creative and transformative. I know of no greater way to tap into the very nature of creativity than praying in, through and by the Holy Spirit. There are numerous scriptures which teach us about prayer; however, the passage which helped me put the missing link of the puzzle together was Romans 8:26.

In Romans 8:26, Paul shows us that we cannot pray by ourselves. How many of you have started out in prayer and five minutes later, you feel as if you are done? There is a longing to pray, but you don't have the will power, the words or the strength to continue. The truth is you don't. This is exactly why Paul said, "the Spirit...helps our weakness; for we do not know how to pray as we should, but the Spirit Himself intercedes for us..." The problem is that we have not given the Holy Spirit His rightful place in our prayer lives.

Whole chapters in John are given to the Holy Spirit, and the book of Acts has been termed the "Acts of the Holy Spirit." Jesus told His disciples to not do anything until they were endued with

Discovering, Developing and Expanding the Real You

power from on high, and Paul in Ephesians 5:18 instructs us to be "filled with the Spirit." It is the Holy Spirit who empowers us with gifts (I Corinthians 12:4-11), and it is by His powerful influence upon our hearts that we are able to display the very fruit of Christ's character (Galatians 5:22).

As we are looking at the Spirit and prayer, we need to turn back to the book of Romans. Romans Chapter 8 is one of those chapters dedicated to explaining and emphasizing the work of the Holy Spirit. There are 16 direct references made in this one chapter concerning the Spirit. This chapter alone should convince us that without the Holy Spirit, we couldn't live as Christ would have us to live.

The emphasis I want to place on this chapter is the needed aid of the Holy Spirit in prayer. Although we have been placed into Christ and adopted as sons and daughters of God, it is the Spirit who aids so that we can pray as we should.

Jesus has gone away physically as He said He would; however, He has not left us without His aid. As we renew our minds with the word of God and allow the Holy Spirit to fill our hearts through prayer, we awaken to the realization that we are seated in Heavenly places with Him. Our spirit, which has been made in His likeness and image, is joined and made one with the very same Spirit that raised Him from the dead (Romans 8:11). As I realized how much I needed the Holy Spirit, I sought to be filled with more of the Holy Spirit.

Jesus promised us that He would baptize us with the Holy Spirit and fire. We see in Acts 2 that the church was brought to birth through the outpouring of the Holy Spirit. From the conception of the body of Christ, it has been empowered with the creativity of the Spirit of life for the fulfilling of its mission. How much more do you think we need the Spirit as we are coming to the end of the age?

It is of utmost importance that we tap into the very creative mind of Christ for the fulfilling of His purpose through our lives. It does not matter what we have been called to do we need his

Discovering, Developing and Expanding the Real You

creative wisdom and power at work in our lives, businesses, churches actually all that we do.

We must become a Spirit-filled people! I personally do not hold to a traditional Pentecostal theology, which believes the evidence of receiving the baptism in the Holy Spirit is speaking in tongues. I do believe the evidence of the baptism in the Holy Spirit is **the evidence of the power of God** actively working in our lives and within that package will come the availability to speak in tongues.

You may say this is simply a play on words, but I believe scripture puts the emphasis on the power of God actively at work in our lives as evidence that we have been baptized in the Holy Spirit. However, the Bible also gives importance to the manifestations of the Spirit at work in our lives (I Corinthians 14:1) and the spiritual power of praying in tongues during our personal devotion to our Father.

I understand this is a controversial subject in some circles. I am okay if you take a different position, but I am writing from my personal experience and clearly Paul's personal experience. He gave a whole chapter to clarify what was then and even now a confusing subject.

When you start talking about the Holy Spirit it can be somewhat subjective, and everyone experiences Him in varying ways in their lives. I don't propose clearing up the controversy, but I am going to teach you what I see the scriptures teach. The place of the Holy Spirit's active participation is of necessity for each of us to fulfill the will of the Father in the same way that it was for the Pattern Son – Jesus Christ.

It has been my personal experience that, aided by the power of praying in the Spirit, prayer takes on a whole new dimension. Yes, we can pray in, by and through the Spirit without praying in tongues. However, if you read I Corinthians 14 Paul discusses his use of tongues in both public and private use. Paul, in his discussion with the Corinthian church concerning tongues, told them, "I thank God, I SPEAK IN TONGUES MORE THAN YOU ALL; however in the church I desire to speak five words

Discovering, Developing and Expanding the Real You

with my mind that I may instruct others also" (I Cor. 14:18-19). (Emphasis Mine)

Paul in no way was teaching against tongues but was putting it in its proper place depending on the context. Paul was not discouraging the Corinthians from speaking in tongues but was instructing them in its proper use. He said in verse 14, "if I pray in a tongue, my spirit prays, but my mind is unfruitful," and in verse 15, "What is the outcome then? I shall pray with the spirit; and I shall pray with the mind also; I shall sing with the spirit and I shall sing with the mind also." Praying in tongues is for personal edification, and it is the aiding power of the Holy Spirit helping us in our spiritual walk.

Romans 8:27 says, "He who searches the hearts knows what the mind of the Spirit is, because He intercedes for the saints ACCORDING TO THE WILL OF GOD" (Emphasis Mine). The Holy Spirit joins our spirit in praying the very mind of Christ. This is why Paul said, "I pray with my spirit and I pray with my understanding." When we pray in tongues, our spirit is being edified and built up through the Holy Spirit.

It is the Holy Spirit who helps us pray accurately. We are limited in our understanding, but the Holy Spirit knows the will of God. Every time you spend 30 minutes praying you are praying out the purpose of God. At the same time, the Holy Spirit will bring revelation to you so you can pray in your understanding. This takes us beyond our limited understanding of prayer so that by the Holy Spirit, we tap into the very mind of Christ.

The Holy Spirit will give us answers to problems in our family, work, ministries, cities, etc. We need the revelation of the Spirit of God to see beyond our own understanding since the essence of creativity flows out of our hearts under the inspiration of the Spirit.

I have gone through this doctrinal explanation to establish a foundation of the importance of the Spirit of God in our daily lives. Prayer is the breath of God that inspires us to think beyond human understanding into the very thoughts of heaven.

Discovering, Developing and Expanding the Real You

If you look at the back of this book in Appendix B, I have listed and explained the manifestations of the Holy Spirit. The revelatory manifestations of the Spirit are the word of wisdom and word of knowledge; along with the interpretation of tongues. All of this ties in with the creative nature of God. As we pray in the Spirit, the manifestations of the Spirit will be more active in our lives. We will have wisdom beyond human wisdom and knowledge beyond human knowledge. It is the kingdom of God coming into this earth through our thought patterns as we pray in the Spirit. We become partners with heaven and an extension of His creative heart.

The Spirit of Christ is the very source of creative wisdom. It is only as we surrender our hearts to the identity of the cross and learn to align them to the nature of Christ that our true potential is released. Romans 8:7 says that "the mind set on the flesh is hostile toward God." Surrender is the key to a life governed by the Spirit of God and a key to successfully living the life of creativity.

The same Spirit that turned water into wine is the same Spirit that will give us the creative power to make wise decisions, have clear direction, invent things, heal the sick, give prophetic words, etc. He is not limited to what we consider spiritual things but is involved in every area of our lives if we give Him place.

George Washington Carver was a black man born in 1864, just one year before the Civil War ended, and his influence can still be felt upon this nation. Carver's reputation is based on his research into and promotion of alternatives to cotton crops, such as peanuts, soybeans and sweet potatoes. These alternative crops also aided in nutrition for farm families.

George Washington Carver wanted poor farmers to grow alternative crops both as a source for their own food and as a source of additional products for improving their quality of life. The most popular of his 44 practical bulletins for farmers contained 105 food recipes using peanuts. He also developed and promoted about 100 products made from peanuts that were useful for the house and farm, including cosmetics, dyes, paints, plastics, gasoline and nitroglycerin.

Carver was a man of prayer, and he believed that the Spirit of God would speak to him. He was quoted as saying, [7]"I indulge in very little lip service but ask the Great Creator silently, daily, and often many times a day to permit me to speak to Him through the three great kingdoms of the world which He created--the animal, mineral, and vegetable kingdoms--to understand their relations to each other, and our relations to them and to the Great God who made all of us." Is it any wonder that this man's life transformed agriculture forever in America and made him instrumental in causing us to be the breadbasket of the world?

WE ADVANCE BY THE CREATIVE POWER OF THE SPIRIT

In my experience, I have seen that we have had the manifestations of the Spirit in operation, but for too much of the time, we have focused on manifestations in a meeting and not the practical application of the Spirit into daily life. If we want to succeed, we must flow with the Holy Spirit in all the details of life and allow His manifestations in whatever we are doing.

It was John Wimber who wrote the bestselling book *Power Evangelism*. The essence of the book is about the church advancing and expanding when the Holy Spirit is actively involved in our preaching and sharing. It also documents how the manifestations of the Spirit (I Corinthians 12, Appendix B) are a key to seeing the church push back the kingdom of darkness.

If the power of the Holy Spirit is to help us advance and expand, then shouldn't that apply to all areas of our lives given that the church is a multi-faceted body? If you are a doctor, wouldn't it be beneficial to have the ultimate Healer at work with you on a daily basis? How about if you are a lawyer? Wouldn't you want to have the Spirit of Truth in all that you decide? To have the Holy Spirit actively involved with all that we do, we have to earnestly desire His participation.

Paul instructed us in I Corinthians 14:1 to earnestly desire the

Discovering, Developing and Expanding the Real You

Spirit's place in our lives. "Earnestly desiring" is something in which we should all be actively participating. To earnestly desire means that we will devote serious effort or energy to attain. If you want to succeed in the kingdom, you must give yourself to the Spirit's ability. You have a certain gift set, but it is the Spirit's ability that takes you beyond just relying on your gift and relying on the Spirit's ability through you.

LIVING A LIFE GOVERNED BY THE SPIRIT

Out of the darkness or obscurity God spoke all things into existence. We serve a creative God. He is behind all forms of art and creative genius. Within each of us is creativity to accomplish the will of God.

It was Martin Luther King Jr. who said, "If a man is called to be a street sweeper, he should sweep streets even as Michelangelo painted, or Beethoven composed music, or Shakespeare wrote poetry. He should sweep streets so well that all the hosts of heaven and earth will pause to say, here lived a great street sweeper who did his job well." You can only paint your picture in this life with all of the color it deserves if you give your whole heart to the ultimate Creator in whom unlimited creativity is found.

As you probably know by now, I love the book of Romans. Romans 8:14 says, "as many as are led by the Spirit of God, these are sons of God." The little word *led* in the original Greek actually means to be led, ruled or governed. We all talk about Jesus being the head of the church, and He is our representative head. However, He administers His rule through the Holy Spirit. Hopefully, I've already shown you enough of the Bible to validate this point. Just for you naysayers, let's take a look at one more scripture.

In II Corinthians 3, Paul discusses how the Spirit's active role is causing us to be living letters written by the work of the Spirit upon our hearts. He ends this chapter by saying in verse 17, "Now the Lord is the Spirit and where the Spirit of the Lord is, there is

Discovering, Developing and Expanding the Real You

liberty." Yes, this scripture says, "the Lord is the Spirit." The Spirit of God is the representative of the Godhead in this earth, and it is His activity in our lives that directs, empowers, convicts, corrects, heals, speaks through us, etc.

Jesus sets the example of a Spirit-led life. If you look in the book of Acts, you will notice that the Spirit, in fulfilling the will of God through the disciples, directed them by His Spirit. I can't tell you the number of times I have been directed by the Sprit in fulfilling the will of God in ministering to others, in a business transaction, in school, in my family, etc.

I recall one of those amazing times I had as a missionary in Africa. I had just spent time in Zambia and was traveling through Zimbabwe to South Africa. Zambia is a poor country, and I could not leave with anything. I literally gave them all the money and clothes I had. The church where I ministered made me some traditional African clothing, and other than a backpack, that was all I had. Because I had no money or food, I was planning on fasting for the two-day train ride.

I boarded the train in Victoria Falls, Zimbabwe. The train had four bunks to a room. I took the top bunk, and another man took the one below me. I began to talk to the man in the lower bunk, and he handed me enough money to eat food for my entire trip to South Africa. I never told the man I had no money--he happened to be a Spirit-filled businessman traveling to a conference.

Two days later the train arrived in far north South Africa, and I got off the train at 2:00 a.m. in the dark. I had no phone and only knew the name of the man I was supposed to contact to take me down south. There were benches at the train station, so I lay down and went to sleep.

After a few hours, I heard people walking all around me. Keep in mind, I am a white man dressed in African attire in north South Africa, and Apartheid had only been abolished one year earlier. To help you understand this context, white people did not sleep out in the open, and they surely did not wear African attire. I stood up and a crowd of Africans gathered around me.

I did not say anything when some started telling me I looked like Jesus. Well, I could not have set up a better opportunity. You got it. I preached the gospel and gave an invitation for salvation. Hands went up all over the place. I spent time praying, and the train came and took the crowd away.

Chapter 5

Networking: The Key To Expansion

"The kingdom of heaven is like a dragnet thrown into the sea."

~ Matthew 13:47 ~
The Lexham English Bible

We are living in an age of interconnectedness as never before: the worldwide web, e-mail and cell phones just to name a few. We can watch sports, and many other events live on TV and, sadly, even war. We can arrange a bus trip, train trip or airline flight instantly via the Internet. We can accomplish all of this because there is a network in place that makes it all a reality.

Revolution would be the only adequate word to describe the transition we are in right now regarding technology and it is changing the way we do business, experience church and transforming entire societies. [8] "The new digital democracy that technology ushers in is also realigning the way we organize ourselves. Things are getting more fluid, less centralized, more interpersonal. The digital era, with the associated network thinking and acting, sets us up to experience movement again in a significant way."

On the shores of Galilee, Jesus spoke to the people who were gathered to listen, and He skillfully painted a picture in their minds of the huge dragnets that were commonly used in that day. It was this image that Jesus used to explain the kingdom of God.

[9] "The dragnet was made up of thousands of connecting knots, which held the net together and made it an amazing tool. The netting was shaped like a long wall 300 feet long and 12 feet high. The bottom of the net had weights with sinkers and the top rope had cork floats. The net was folded. A team of up to 16 men held the strong rope attached to the dragnet.

A second boat and team of men sailed out with the other end of the net. When the net was fully stretched, the boat circled around and came back to shore, where the team alighted and held the ropes. Both teams then dragged the net and its contents back to the shore. This method enabled the fishermen to catch the fish that were hiding out at the bottom of the lake. The fish were then handed over to be sorted, and the operation was performed again-- as many as eight times in one day."

It was this picture of the dragnet that Jesus used in this parable to show how our interconnectedness is the way we expand our reach. If you want to expand, you must be connected to the right systems and people.

DEVELOP YOUR NICHE

The word *niche* is derived from the French word *nicher*, meaning *to nest*. The term was coined by the naturalist Joseph Grinnell in 1917. The Grinnellian niche concept embodies the idea that the niche of a species is determined by the habitat in which it lives. The word is still used by ecologists, but it has now been adapted into the mainstream of our vernacular through the business world. The concept of niche brands, products and marketing has revolutionized our way of expanding our reach in the marketplace.

When you ask most businesspeople or even ministries who their audience is, they usually give you the pat answer, "anyone."

Discovering, Developing and Expanding the Real You

Is it any wonder many of them are not hitting their target? The reality is that you must understand who you are if you want to network and market yourself accurately.

It is only by truly defining yourself that you can get a strategy. Jesus was very specific in His purpose because He knew who He was. He crafted His message to His audience because He always knew His target. If you want to be authentic in reaching others, you must know who you are which will translate into knowing exactly who your audience is.

I hope to reveal concepts that you can use in any situation-- from networking with those who are like-minded homeschoolers to a service business to being a church planter. Basic principles apply to those who are hungry to expand their influence, but if you are satisfied with where you are, I am reaching the wrong target. I want to help those who want to change this world, whether you are a mother homeschooling your child or the young man wanting to change this world by being a church planter. The key thing that separates you from the crowd is that you are a hungry disciple who wants to be a changer of the world around you.

If you want to expand your reach, you must build relationships with like-minded networkers. The very reason you need to know who you are is to be able to connect with others for encouragement, counsel, new ideas, diversification and expansion.

You can utilize your resources and time by going to the right conferences and trade shows or by reading the right material which will keep you focused on the things that will propel you forward. It is only when you know exactly who your audience is that you can be very specific. Knowing your niche market opens the minds of your networking partners and makes their job of referring people to you much easier.

I have a friend who started a home school network. They had a disagreement with the group as to their target market. One faction wanted to be exclusive to those who had the same doctrinal positions while the other faction wanted a more open group to include the entire community. I am not saying which position is correct, either position can be taken, but you do have to define yourself so that those with like interest can know who you are, where you are going and what you are doing.

If you have a church with a coffee house and people who have a very expressive worship style, your target audience is not going to be older people who are more traditional and set in their ways. Don't waste your time or be discouraged because you are not reaching everyone. You are not going to. Focus on your target audience and you will expand into the consistent sustainable growth for which your enterprise is destined.

ORGANIC EXPANSION

I think I can confidently say that we all want to see growth come to whatever we are doing. If we don't, then we aren't living because every living thing is growing and expanding. In today's corporate, environmental and sociological communities, all the rage is sustainability. In looking at that this from an economical viewpoint, sustainability is a term used to identify various strategies that make it possible to utilize available resources to their best advantage.

I want to use the idea of economic sustainability in the context of my audience. If you are reading this book, you are more than likely not the corporate CEO or mega church pastor, but just you attempting to be you. I am convinced that we are living in the day when the new big is small.

Neil Cole, whom I consider to be one of the prolific thinkers of our time in the church world, sums up the whole concept of organic growth thusly: "Why is small so big? Small does not cost a lot. Small is easy to reproduce. Small is more easily changed and exchanged. Small is mobile. Small is harder to stop. Small is intimate. Small is simple. Small infiltrates easier. We can change the world more quickly by becoming much smaller in our strategy." Networking is learning to combine the many smalls into a strategic purpose that makes them a force with which to be reckoned.

Discovering, Developing and Expanding the Real You

When you are a small or medium sized enterprise, it is much easier to serve the needs of your followers, clients and purchasers. The reason is because you can be more intimate and focused; you can meet their needs more effectively. When you can do this, growth is more natural and sustainable because you can utilize your resources based on real needs instead of perceived needs. You can change your direction much more quickly. By that I mean if you are building relationships, you are getting feedback from those you are serving; therefore, you can build products, services or churches to effectively reach people where they need help.

I am not saying that a big business or church cannot do this because there are those who do. I think of companies like Amazon and Apple who provide great service and listen to feedback from their customers. I think of Austin Stone Church in Austin, Texas that is defined as a Mega Church but is striving to accommodate mutual interaction.

However, when you reach a certain size, it is much easier to lose touch with those you are serving if you don't have the right distributive network built into your enterprise. At some point, we have all had to call a major company for assistance only to find ourselves lost in the maze of uncaring workers. In our spiritual walk, many of us have been lost in the mega church where we were a person in the chair and not a vital participant.

God uses the big, but the power of the future is with the small and medium sized interconnected business, non-profit or church growing in its specific ecosystem. We are going through a major paradigm shift as to how we interact, and that shift in power is moving from the "Mega" to the "Network."

Large churches are increasingly recognizing that the Networking Church model, which involves the collaboration of multiple fellowships, is a more effective and natural approach to addressing individuals' needs and providing opportunities for members to utilize their talents. It emphasizes interdependence and interconnectedness. The Mega church focuses on one big,

centralized entity while the Networking Church is concerned with
expressing church at many different levels, depending on the
environment in which it is ministering.

The advantage of this idea of church is that it can release every
member to grow into the fullest expression of individual ministry
while remaining a functioning part of the whole. It can penetrate
every part of society with expressions like marketplace ministries,
discipleship communities, networks of house churches and
traditional congregational communities with large celebration
gatherings that can impact and transform whole cities and regions.
It allows the church to be the living, breathing organism that the
Holy Spirit created it to be.

During the time the Bible was written, agriculture was a daily
part of people's lives. Jesus frequently used parables from nature
and agriculture to illustrate the nature of the kingdom of God–the
lilies of the field, the seed that grows by itself, the growth of the
mustard seed, the four soils, the tree and its fruit, the laws of
sowing and reaping. In all of these examples, expansion is organic
and can be sustained since it happens naturally. It does not always
happen fast, but growth is consistent and more apt to remain for
the long term.

In looking back at the word *niche*, it is a term that refers to an
ecological system. The niche of a species is determined by the
habitat in which it lives. In other words, the niche is the sum of
the habitat requirements that allow a species to persist and
produce offspring. Isolating your target market is learning their
habitat.

You must study and know the habitat of your ideal customers
as well as you know yourself. If you are a web designer, you may
be marketing to "anyone who needs a new, cutting edge, amazing,
fully optimized website that is the best in the world!" However, if
your expertise is to design websites specifically for medical
providers, it demonstrates that you know that habitat, you know
the industry language and you know the touch and feel for which a
medical provider is looking. You are an expert in that field and
medical customers are going to have confidence in you because

Discovering, Developing and Expanding the Real You

you know their habitat.

FIND YOUR VOICE

We all have been around the young man going through puberty whose voice begins to crack and change. It is a very awkward time, but it is a necessary change to becoming a man. In addition to bodily changes, emotional changes occur causing a redirection of focus from childlike thinking to more independent thinking. What happens in the midst of this change is of utmost importance. We all have to find our voice in this world because our voice is one thing that defines who we are.

The process of finding your voice is similar for an individual or an organization. You must determine for yourself what you are good at and what you enjoy doing since it signifies your personal gifting or your organizational vision. When you find your voice, you are articulating who you are and are no longer emulating someone else.

The only way you or your organization is going to make an impact is to market in a way unique to you. It is not by following some expert's rules or by following the herd but by doing it in the way that works for you. The only way you can distinguish yourself is to be yourself.

The process of finding your voice is explained in the introduction of this book as the "independent stage" of growth. It is a time of trial and error to push the boundaries to discover yourself then develop what you have discovered. You have to be willing to take chances.

Just think about what Steve Jobs did with Apple while he was alive. He found his voice and sang a song that others followed, but he had to be willing to take chances. If you want to distinguish yourself or distinguish your organization, then sing the tune that fits you, sing it loudly and be willing to risk the chance for ridicule.

DEVELOP YOUR MESSAGE

It is not enough to find your voice, but you must also learn to craft your message. Your message is your life or the life of your organization; you could also call it your brand. I have seen two extremes in the church. There are those who see marketing in a nutshell, "worldly and, therefore, demonic." Then there are those who rely solely on marketing techniques.

Regardless of the approach you take, you have a brand or message whether you clearly define it or not. It goes without saying that if we have a product or message that is worth hearing, shouldn't we make it clear and defined? Because you are going to be defined in the eyes of others anyway, the question is, "what is that message saying?"

Branding is about ownership and a way of establishing who we are. [10]"It allows you to be part of something larger than yourself in the same way that, hundreds of years ago, the Irish and the English and the French identified themselves through their emblems and crests. The hidden emotional truth behind the reach and impact of branding is that people want to belong to something larger than themselves."

Branding and messaging are not about being who you want to be but about being that which you can't help but be. When we adhere to this concept, our voice makes a clear distinct sound. Paul said in I Corinthians 14:7-8 that if lifeless things, like a flute or a harp, do not make clear musical notes, you will not know what is being played. And in a war, if the trumpet does not give a clear sound, who will prepare for battle?

It is the same with you. Let's look at this from a ministry perspective. If you are a teacher, you don't want to market yourself as an evangelist. Branding must be authentic, or it is deceptive and, in the end, will be detrimental instead of expansive.

You must find the inner truth about the message of your product or service. To gain the loyalty and trust of followers, your

Discovering, Developing and Expanding the Real You

message – conveyed through advertising or marketing – has to be authentic. Your message is what you do best because it identifies you or brands you.

We don't have to view marketing and messaging through the eyes of Madison Avenue. We all market in one way or another, just in differing degrees. In simple reality, defining and developing your message is marketing. It is simply defining who you are, what you can do and how you can benefit others. You may have only one attempt to convince someone that you have something to offer them.

Defining your message and brand will help you know what other businesses and organizations to align with. Which trade shows, conferences and meetings target your audience? Which ones offer the ability to utilize your resources to the fullest potential? These are ways of moving you away from the shotgun approach to the approach of a marksman.

Peter and Paul took a different approach in the way they ministered the gospel. Paul's brand was to the Gentile world while Peter's was to the Jewish people. One is not better than the other; it is just about knowing who you are and being comfortable with the way you have been made. Paul understood that he was who he was because of the grace of God. The grace of God upon our lives helps us define our message.

It is only by finding your voice and developing your message that you can define your market. You are only going to find success in your endeavor if you are able to reach your target audience. If our goal is to complete the will of God for our lives, which includes our organizational endeavors, then we have to know our audience.

Jesus understood who He was speaking to and developed His message to reach His particular audience. The way He communicated with His three closest disciples (Peter, James and John) was different than the way He communicated with the five thousand. In developing your message, you might try asking yourself some of the following questions.

- Of all people who could use my product, service, or teaching, who am I most passionate about working with? Who do I most closely identify with? Understand? Even sympathize with?

- Who will benefit the most from what I have to offer?

- If I have to devote a lot of time and effort learning about a particular industry, demographic or subject, which one would I enjoy the most? Which one do I already know the most about?

By answering these questions, you can direct your efforts effectively. Knowing who you are allows you to align with others, learn from them, or become an expert that others seek for guidance. When your message is clear, it is easier for others to seek your expertise, which can benefit both you and those you assist.

YOU NEED A JOHN THE BAPTIST

To expand, you need someone or something to pave the way. Word of mouth is the best marketing strategy; it's cheap, effective, and wide-reaching, but it requires time to develop. Is there any way to accelerate this process?

Like most of us, you probably were not born into a family business or ministry; however, the benefits of such a situation cannot be underestimated and taking advantage of it can be a great asset. For those of us who do not have this benefit, how do we expand our influence in a world overloaded with so many messages? One such tool that has gone a long way in leveling the playing field is the Internet and more specifically, social media.

Social media and Internet marketing can be used to prepare the way so that when you speak, people hear your unique voice and message. I am not opposed to any type of marketing strategy, such as flyers, newspapers, trade shows or even buying local cable or radio time, since you must find what works for you. You will more than likely use a combination of tools.

In today's world, however, social networking is a vital part of

Discovering, Developing and Expanding the Real You

branding yourself. One way to do that if you have a business, ministry or non-profit is to optimize your Facebook landing page, Twitter page and other social media appropriate to your enterprise, along with your blog or website, to ensure your message is clear, concise and relevant to your audience.

It is possible that your endeavor does not require this level of social media networking; therefore, you will have to determine how to connect with others to reach your audience. I have a friend who ministers in prisons, so his audience is somewhat captive. He does utilize social media to connect with others who have similar visions and callings but not to reach his main audience.

The idea of reaching your audience all over the world is absolutely amazing; no other generation has had such an opportunity. This approach has put all types of enterprises out of business, but at the same time, it allows the average person to compete in an arena where an idea can gain traction and grow. You may only be trying to reach a local community, but you can still harness the power of social media as one tool in your box to expand your influence. If you are like my wife and me, who direct Foundation Publications, then the Internet is one of our main tools for exposure.

When you buy a product, go to a church or give to an organization, what do you expect? Do you buy just because you have been pestered? Do you fellowship with others when all they want to do is take? Do you give to an organization with which you are not acquainted? I think there is one common ingredient that we all expect--trust.

We must trust that the product is going to be good and durable; trust that those with whom we fellowship have a common heart, focus and love; trust that when we give to an organization, the funds will be utilized responsibly. How do we build this trust with others so that trust can be the linchpin to expansion? The challenge is learning to effectively build a trustworthy brand that people want what we have to offer. If we can lay these foundations, there will be sustainable growth built around relationships with those whom we are serving.

As I said previously, word of mouth or someone paving the way for you, is the most powerful way to introduce yourself, and developing relationships is the most powerful way to expansion. A friend, mentor, family member or customer can be one of your best assets for expansion. A "John the Baptist" is someone who has confidence in you or your product and will help you spread the word.

In today's world, most of the same people with whom you relate also relate with each other through social media, and we must utilize that platform. It is possible that in ten years we will have moved on to something other than social media, but right now, it is a powerful medium to access. I am not saying we all have to have a Facebook Fan page or X page etc., but I am saying that we need to take advantage of the tools God has provided for us today. Paul the apostle went to the crossroads of the world to get his message out to as many people as possible.

In his book *Launch*, Michael Stelzner reveals a few key ideas in utilizing our personal blog, Facebook, X, Instagram, LinkedIn, or any other social media. The principles apply in varying contexts and can be used outside of social media. They can be used in everything that we do and in any marketing strategy application. Firstly, instead of pestering people with a sales pitch, help them. This will develop a level of trust. If you can show someone that you are not trying to get your hands in their pocket but are there to help them, they are more apt to listen. Secondly, involve others instead of solely focusing on yourself, your products or your services.

[11] "When you combine great content with great people, you quickly stand apart from others in your industry, attracting large numbers of prospective customers. Down the road it will be those people who will propel your business beyond your competitors. The formula is 'great content' plus 'other people' minus 'marketing messages' equals growth.

When you offer great content--such as detailed how-to articles, expert interviews, case studies, and videos that focus on helping

Discovering, Developing and Expanding the Real You

other people solve their problems, you'll experience growth. The 'other' component transcends your reader base and involves reaching out to people outside your company, such as industry experts. All of this transpires in a marketing free zone."

Peter uses a term in II Peter 1:1, "like precious faith." In this context, it is about finding people who share your passion and linking together with them.

SYNERGY THE PATHWAY OF EXPANSION

In the United States, the majority of businesses and churches are classified as small. A small business is classified as 25 or fewer employees; a small church is considered 25 to 150 consistent attendees. Both of these by far make up the majority.

If the majority of businesses and churches are small, it goes without saying that we do not have millions of dollars to promote our endeavor. At the writing of this book, the U.S. automotive industry is spending more than $400 to market each car, and that adds up to $4 billion annually. In the midst of this media onslaught, there are those learning the power of open network systems, along with synergy, to utilize others with similar strengths.

In the book *The Starfish and the Spider*, the authors show how open systems are transforming our world. People contribute in open systems because they believe they have a voice, they can make a difference and their input is valued. Synergy is about networking and harnessing the expertise of others. You can apply this in your congregation, a city government or a business. In I Corinthians 3:6, Paul used this principle when he said, "one plants, one waters, but God brings the increase" (my paraphrase). The principle is learning to value every part and utilize each part for the growth of the whole.

I want to define synergy for you again because I think it truly demonstrates the networking principle. *Synergy is the working together of two things to produce an effect greater than the sum of the parts.* Synergy is unleashed when we combine small things to make something bigger, just like in the parable of the dragnet. If you are a church planter, you can unleash the power of synergy by collaborating with a network of churches. I think many times we try to reinvent the wheel. We have to discover our strengths, but we must be secure enough to utilize and include the strengths of others.

We cannot accurately view the challenges and opportunities in front of us without multiple perspectives. We all have blind spots in our lives and synergy is about being humble enough to problem solve, create vision and strategically plan with others input. [12]"When existing ideas and concepts collide to form new and unusual combinations, they create a spark for innovative thinking to take place."

Building relationships with others is networking. It is how the kingdom is expanded, along with your endeavor. I am not saying that we should not use more traditional forms of marketing, but I am saying that networking will be the most powerful arsenal in the marketing toolbox. You should focus on growing your network base of trust before you start the sales or growing of your church. It may take more time, but it is more cost effective and sustainable in the long term. Build a dragnet that involves others, since it is the key to kingdom expansion.

Chapter 6

Implementation: The Key To Fulfillment

"Everyone who hears these words of mine and does them is like a
wise man who built his house on rock. The rain fell, the flood
came, and the winds beat against that house, but it did not collapse
because it had been founded on rock."

~ Matthew 7:24-25 ~

At the time I was writing this book, I spent the weekend with
a successful doctor. He has been practicing medicine for 40
years and he informed me that most doctors lack simple business
skills. I could include lawyers, preachers and even small
businessmen in this long list of why someone with great skill
many times cannot succeed in the endeavor they undertake.
Wisdom is the ability to fully implement a plan. It is more than
having a skill; it is learning how to practically use a skill in a
constructive way to help yourself and others. Jesus called this
kind of wisdom the ability to build something that will practically
affect this world. It is heaven coming to earth and building upon
the solid rock.

Jesus taught us to pray that the kingdom of God would come to
this earth. The only way the kingdom can be established in this
earth is to put into practice the word of God in our lives.
Knowledge is good, but it does not change us unless it is applied. I
have met many professors who have much knowledge, but their
lives are a mess. Implementation is taking what we know and

Discovering, Developing and Expanding the Real You

putting it into practice.

When I was completing my business degree, one of my professors had a Doctorate's degree in business administration. He was a brilliant guy but guess what?--he had never run a business. He had great ideas and could tell you what had worked for others, but he had no personal experience. We need more than just knowing what is important; we need the wisdom to know how to make it work.

CARPE DIEM

In the movie "Dead Poet's Society," Robin Williams, the unconventional professor, took his students out of their comfort zone and, as an artist, inspired them to seize their moment in time. *Carpe Diem* is Latin for "seize the day"--we can either seize the day or lose the day. How do we lose the day? We lose the day when we allow fear to paralyze us into in inaction.

The only purpose in starting is to finish. If you want to seize your moment, you have to hit the publish button on your blog, do your sales presentation, preach your sermon, open the coffee shop. Seth Godin in his book *Indispensable* says, "Shipping something out the door, doing it regularly, without hassle, emergency, or fear – this is a rare skill, something that makes you indispensable."

We all have gifts and creative ability within us to accomplish the will of God, but it takes going against your fear of failure and stepping out of the boat to get to your stated goals. You have an indispensable place in God's plan, but you must be willing to put action to your plan. It is comfortable to stay in the boat and let someone else take the risk. However, if you are not willing to take the risk, you don't get the reward either.

Discipleship is about seizing the moment. You really can't call yourself a disciple if you are unwilling to take risks. I can hear some now—*"Darren, you are being too radical."* Am I? What did Jesus say to his disciples? If you are really serious about seizing the moment, search the scriptures and find what Jesus said to those who became His disciples. I guarantee you it changed

Discovering, Developing and Expanding the Real You

their lives forever. (To learn more read or listen to Lesson 38: The Demand Of The Kingdom, wwwfoundaitonpub.org.)

Pursuing the will of God does not always look like the right path. Think about Moses who went from the second in command of Egypt to a shepherd in the desert for 40 years. Seizing the moment can mean many different things depending on the season we are in during our life's journey. The ways of God sometimes require that we go down before we go up. It is the process of allowing God to empty us of our own agenda so He can fill us with His agenda. In the end, it is His agenda that will prevail. That is what I want, and I am sure that is what you want, too.

How we finish is what really matters. In the introduction of this book, I stated that the will of God matures in stages. We need to be willing to seize the moment in each stage. Success is completing the will of God in each season of our life, and that may look different than the way many people view success.

Moses was a success on the backside of the desert. It was his obedience in every stage that led to the ultimate fulfillment of God's will. Stop trying to figure everything out; stop comparing yourself with everyone else and simply do what you need to do in this season. Yes, remember your ultimate vision and the goals you have set, but also remember that you may have to take a step back before you can go forward.

Seizing your moment is never stopping and putting into practice your game plan. Fear of failure is the only thing keeping you from going forward. At times, it will feel like you work all day or night and have nothing to show for it at the end of the day. The real key, however, is to get rid of the idea that the payoff for hard work is always going to be smooth and easy. Sometimes it rains, even pours. Some days are dry, even parched and feel more like the desert. It is imperative to maintain a consistent, systematic approach and work your plan every day, repeatedly until you reap in due season.

The reality is that completion ultimately comes to people who work consistently and refuse to be deterred or discouraged when

Discovering, Developing and Expanding the Real You

instant gratification does not happen. Failure is what we many times experience along the pathway of success. However, we only fail when we choose to quit and throw in the towel. I want to encourage you to seize your moment every day. Today is a day that you can affect, and it is by taking the needed steps that will help you get to the place that you are headed. You can't let the fear of failure paralyze you into inaction.

PUT YOUR GOALS TO WORK

Developing an action plan is an important step in the process of putting into action your dreams and goals. An action plan is a roadmap to help you succeed in fulfilling the will of God. It is important to develop an action plan. In chapter 2, I took you through the process of writing a mission statement and personal vision for six areas of your life. An action plan helps you create actual steps in implementing the direction you have determined to take.

We could call the steps we need to take goals. A goal is simply something we use to let us know we are progressing in our desired direction. A goal is a signpost letting us know we have reached a certain destination. I have discovered that without goals, most people procrastinate to the point of forgetting where they are headed, get lost and quit.

I know that some will say this sounds just like self-help combined with business techniques and not the gospel. I will challenge you on that and ask *"didn't Jesus have goals?"* He stated that He came to seek and save that which was lost. He had one focus and that was the Father's goals. He said I have bread to eat that you don't know about, which was doing the will of God. Jesus knew why He came to the earth, His mission and the fulfillment or ultimate goal of that mission. Shouldn't we at least attempt to be as focused as He was?

It is important to make goals clear and simple. Define your goal in such a way that a stranger can read it and know when you've achieved it. When we do this, we move out of a place of

Discovering, Developing and Expanding the Real You

just dreaming about the direction we are headed and put action to our thoughts and dreams. You can fulfill the calling of God upon your life if you are willing to "seize the day."

I want to take you through an exercise that many businesses and personal training courses use called S.M.A.R.T goals. I am going to use myself as a case in point to show you the process I used to write this book. You can apply this exercise to anything you want to accomplish, such as losing weight, finishing a degree, planting a church or starting a business.

The "S" in S.M.A.R.T. stands for **Specific**. A specific goal has a much greater chance of accomplishing than a general goal. To set a specific goal, ask yourself:

Who: Who is involved?

What: What do I want to accomplish?

Where: Identify a location (it may not be a physical location, a Facebook Page or a web-based business.)

When: Establish a time frame.

Which: Identify requirements and constraints.

Why: Specify reasons, purposes or benefits of accomplishing the goal.

A few goals that I charted for myself in writing this particular book project are shown here. It is a simple exercise that you can use for all types of activity, and it helps you to actually put meat on your dreams. If you want to be more than a dreamer and put action to your dreams, you need to start with some concrete steps.

General Goals	Specific Goals
Write a book	Write a book on gifts and how to practically apply them.
Finish the book by January	Write two hours daily

Discovering, Developing and Expanding the Real You

Find an editor	Interview different editors by October
Book cover design	Find a good designer for $500 per book cover.
Include others to give their input on their expertise	Contact experts to write their story for inclusion at the end of each chapter completed.
Print the book	Get manuscript ready to the Needed specifications for uploading to Amazon.com.
Market my book	Set up book signings, ask for speaking engagements, get the word out on social media

The "M" in S.M.A.R.T. stands for **Measurable**. You must establish concrete criteria for measuring your progress toward the attainment of each of your goals. When you measure your progress, you stay on track, reach your target dates and experience the great feeling of achievement that spurs you on to the continued effort required to reach your goal. To determine if your goal is measurable, ask questions such as how much, how many and how long will it take to reach my goal?

The "A" in S.M.A.R.T. stands for **Attainable**. When you identify goals that fit your gift set and calling, you begin to figure out ways to make them happen. You discover and develop the abilities, skills and financial capacity to reach them.

The "R" in S.M.A.R.T. stands for **Relevant**. Is your goal relevant to your life purpose? Is it in line with your beliefs and values? Your action plan must be consistent with your other established goals, and it must fit within your immediate and long-term plans.

The "T" in S.M.A.R.T. stands for **Tangible**. When your goal is tangible, or when you tie an intangible goal to a tangible goal, you have a better chance of making it specific and measurable and thus attainable.

Discovering, Developing and Expanding the Real You

Intangible goals are your desires for internal changes, such as consistency or self-control that are required to reach more tangible goals. Intangible goals are the character changes and behavior patterns you must develop to pave the way to reach a measurable tangible goal, such as losing twenty-five pounds. For example, the intangible goal is self-control while the tangible goal that you can measure is the twenty-five pounds.

What are some of the possible obstacles to your goals? When you know what to expect, you can plan realistically for overcoming or working around any obstacles. In the military, they do what are called war game scenarios. When you start considering likely obstacles, you can then formulate possible solutions or actions for overcoming them.

Selecting the most effective course of action requires considering constraints such as budget, preferences of other team members, and evolving needs and trends. Addressing these constraints in advance will significantly influence your decision-making process during critical moments, which are inevitable in any venture.

If you want to implement it, you have to move from concept to reality, and reality has a time frame. You should list the exact daily actions you must take to bring your goal to reality. Goals depend on the completion of a series of action steps that must be taken in a consecutive order – one after another. You must also set a final target date and write it down. When you post it on the wall or put it on your fridge, the reality of achievement becomes more real. If you want to hit your target, you must have enough nerve to pull the trigger and put action to your preparation.

Now that you know what will be required in time, effort and money to reach your goal, ask yourself an important question: Is it worth the time, effort and money required to reach this goal? If your answer is "Yes," go to work. If your answer is "No," you can discard the goal without feeling a nagging doubt about what you should have done. If you realize that the goal does not fit your values, needs, gifts, motivations or current priorities, your goal could just be a vain imagination. It is your right and responsibility to discard it. However, sometimes your answer to this important question is "Yes, but later."

In the context of your gifting, you may be more of a person who supports. If you remember back in Chapter 2, I made a distinction between leadership and management. If you are a worship leader, you can use this to set goals on how to improve, expand and train others in the context of supporting a larger vision. It is about discovering your place, developing that place and expanding it. What you do in this season may be what you do in the next, but it could just as easily be a training ground.

THE ART OF IMPLEMENTATION

Implementation is more of an art than a science. You can have all of your ducks in a row, but you need the direction of the Spirit to put it all together. Unless the Lord builds the house, we labor in vain (Psalms 127:1). We don't want to just be doing something; we want to be about the Father's business. Fulfilling His plan for our lives must be our greatest desire. We all have a limited amount of time; therefore, let's make sure that what we feel inspired to accomplish is true to who we are, our calling, our gifts and the season of our lives.

In implementing your plan, draw on all available resources and as much as you can, involve people who have the expertise that you need. You don't have to know everything, but it's important to know people who have knowledge in a particular area. You also need to be able to access other resources to get the information you need to fully implement your plan.

One thing we need to do continually is pray that we have the Spirit of wisdom in our hearts. Implementation is about building and wisdom is what gives us the skill to implement the plans, goals, and actions to accomplish our calling.

Wisdom is not something tangible. By that I mean you can't get information out of a book that says here is wisdom step one, step two and step three--now you have it. Wisdom is the ability of

Discovering, Developing and Expanding the Real You

the Spirit directing you through the moment. It is the ability to make a decision that can make or break the endeavor you are undertaking. So many times, we want someone to tell us exactly what to do.

Wisdom is the ability to forge your own path, to discover a route from one place to another that hasn't been paved, measured and quantified. The path of wisdom is the Spirit's path for the moment and that may change from moment to moment because the purpose of God is fluid and grows in stages.

Wisdom is the ability to apply truth so that our lives work the way that they were created to work. We have been created in Christ to do good works (Ephesians 2:10). Wisdom is not limited to knowledge, but it taps into the very heart of God to bring solutions and restoration.

Isaiah 11:2, in speaking about Christ, lists the sevenfold anointing. One of the characteristics is not to judge by the seeing of our eyes or the hearing of our ears. Wisdom is an inner listening to the heart as the Spirit speaks, guides and leads. It is more like intuition rather than getting information by reading a manual. You can study all the plans you need in order to put your action plans in place, but ultimately you must cultivate a listening heart to be able to see how the plan will come together as it should.

We can't look ahead and see everything, but the Spirit of God knows the end from the beginning and the best path to get us to our destination. It could appear sensible for us to take the four-lane road to get us quickly to our destination, but sometimes the Spirit will lead us on a detour through the back roads. Why? There may be an accident ahead, we may not be ready to get to our destination or there may be someone that needs help on that back road.

We are in this system; therefore, we need wisdom to navigate through life's circumstances. Wisdom can be defined as the ability to relate with God and others. It can also be defined as the ability to do the right thing at the right time or the ability to understand

Discovering, Developing and Expanding the Real You

what to avoid doing. The book of Proverbs defines wisdom as the
principal thing or the main thing (Proverbs 8:29-30, 9:1).

Wisdom makes us adaptable. In today's world, one thing we
must be is adaptable. Having the wisdom to know what to stick
with or discard can mean your very survival. What do you do if
you are in a plane that has lost one engine, is carrying a lot of
cargo and is heading for a mountain? With one engine out, you
are unable to get over the mountain with all the weight that you
have. You start unloading the unnecessary cargo so you can get
the lift you need to get over the mountain.

Wisdom is the ability to know what you can change and what
you can't, thereby allowing you to put your effort and time into
changeable situations. [13]"There's a difference between passively
accepting every element of your environment (and thus missing
opportunities to exploit) and being wise enough to leave the
unchangeable alone, or at least work around it."

In his book *Linchpin*, Seth Godin tells a story illustrating the
power of implementation. He relates how Richard Branson, who
founded Virgin Airlines, was faced with a decision to either accept
his circumstances or change them. He was at an airport in the
Caribbean when his flight was cancelled--the only flight all day.
In similar situations, people tend to freak out and demand to have
changed what can't be changed. Instead of doing that, Richard
Branson chose to be adaptable.

Branson went to the other side of the airport and inquired about
the cost of chartering an airplane. He then borrowed a portable
blackboard and wrote, "Seats to Virgin Islands, $39." He went
back to his gate with his sign and sold enough airfare to pay for
the flight. When we tap into wisdom, we not only solve our
problems, but we help others along our journey.

Implementation is both a science and an art. It is a science in
the sense that you are dealing with hard facts that need to be
organized, prioritized and put in place. As an art, it is active and,
on the move, always changing, being led more by intuition than
facts. You can't be too dogmatic when it comes to implementation
because sometimes it works just because it works, and a workable

Discovering, Developing and Expanding the Real You

solution is what implementation is all about.

Discovering, Developing and Expanding the Real You

Chapter 7

Perseverance: The Key To Overcoming

"Now we want each of you to demonstrate the same diligence for the
final realization of your hope, so that you won't become lazy but will be
imitators of those who inherit the promises
through faith and perseverance."

~ Hebrews 6:11-12 ~
The Holmann Christian Standard

In one of the greatest expansions of the early church, one of its
premier leaders left us with a mouth full of wisdom. In the
churches that had just been planted, Paul told the new disciples,
*"that through many tribulations we must enter into the kingdom of
God"* (Acts 14:22). Can you imagine? You have just received
eternal life, and the encouraging words that you get are that you
should look forward to and embrace tribulation.

Let's look at this word "tribulation," which means pressure.
Pressure makes diamonds, and it also develops character. We can
have expansion, but it will only be sustained on the bedrock of
solid character.

The reality of character is that it does not come cheap. It will
cost you. It is formed in the test of your faith through hardship
and struggle. [14] "It is worth the cost, but you will have to count
the cost often if you are to attain solid character. Character is
within. Who you are will determine what you do and what you
say. Who you are is more important than anything else, for from it

Discovering, Developing and Expanding the Real You

flows all else" (Proverbs 4:23, Matthew 15:11, 17-20).

I began this book by helping you discover your gifts and calling. I hope at this point you have begun to at least seek the Lord concerning the gifts He has given you and your purpose in using them to their fullest potential. However, if character is not the bedrock upon which we use our gifts, then we are sure to abuse them and hurt others in the process.

THE FOUNDATION OF CHARACTER

I think all of us have seen gifted people display bad character. It really puts a stain on all that they do. It is not my intention to look at others and point fingers or else that finger may be pointing back at me. I want us to look at our own lives so that when we step into His purpose, we don't wind up in a ditch bringing dishonor to our calling and hurting others.

Jesus is our pattern. We see that He was tested and proven before He was released into the fullness of His purpose. If we have not gone through fires in our lives, we will most certainly not be able to handle the pressure that comes with the calling of God. I have found the greater the calling; the more fire will be applied, since it takes time to prepare you for what you are called to do. It does not mean that you will be idle. It does mean that much of what you are doing is simply preparation for your ultimate purpose.

Let's take a look at David, the man after God's own heart. At the age of ten, David received a prophetic word concerning his purpose, but it was not until he was thirty that he was crowned king in Hebron. It took seven more years before he achieved his ultimate calling as king in Jerusalem. If you are in a hurry just sit back because testing takes time.

Character is not given freely like gifts, but it is forged in the furnace of trials. Trust me, I wish there was another way. Have you prayed, *"God make me into the person you want me to be? I want everything you have for my life. Let your kingdom come in my life as it is in heaven?"* He hears your prayer and answers that

Discovering, Developing and Expanding the Real You

prayer, but the pathway is not of your choosing; it's His.

The foundation of character must be forged when the heat is turned up. Adversity is not what we cherish, but it is, ironically, our best friend because it makes us stronger. Paul told us to "rejoice in our sufferings, knowing that suffering produces endurance, and endurance produces character, and character produces hope, and hope does not put us to shame, because God's love has been poured into our hearts through the Holy Spirit who has been given to us" (Romans 5:3-5).

A strong character is built through trials and suffering, not ease and quiet. This is what James taught us when he said to "count it all joy, my brethren, when ye fall into manifold temptations; knowing that the proving of your faith worketh patience. And let patience have its perfect work, that ye may be perfect and entire, lacking in nothing." (James 1:2-4)

YOU CAN'T FINISH IF YOU STOP

I would not call myself an expert runner but have run and do run 5K races. You know, if you stop running in the middle of the race, it does not count. In our modern world, we have forgotten the aspect of discipline and sacrifice. In today's reality, when things get tough, we often fall apart and quit. We lack perseverance. Perseverance is defined as "*steady persistence in a course of action, a purpose, a state etc., especially in spite of difficulties, obstacles, or discouragement.*"

Today, we want everything instant. We have instant potatoes, instant coffee, and people want instant success. If it does not happen quickly, then it can't be God. I have seen in my experience that God doesn't have any shortcuts. The enemy wanted to give Jesus shortcuts in the wilderness, but He refused to take them. God's love was demonstrated to Israel by leading them through the wilderness.

Israel was not ready for ruling; they had to first be tested. If you think there is another way, try to find it. What you will find is that you are going to go around that mountain one more time until you learn the lesson you need to learn.

The wilderness is not our promised land, but we have to go through it to get to where we need to go. Don't camp out in the wilderness but keep moving on so you can finish. On this side of the second coming of Christ, we live in an environment of adversity. Wishing for change does not alter reality. I informed my son early on that life presents challenges. It is important to remember that success requires hard work and time, a lesson that previous generations have understood.

THE PATHWAY TO SUCCESS IS PAVED WITH FAILURE

Michael Jordan once said, "I've failed over and over and over again in my life and that is why I succeed." Failure and success are opposites, right? Isn't this how most of us think? Failures, we reason, are painted black while successes are painted white. They are two diverse paths; paths that will not and cannot intersect. If we look at things like that, we are not looking at the whole picture. Did you know:

- In his early years, teachers told Thomas Edison he was "too stupid to learn anything." He invented the light bulb.
- Albert Einstein did poorly in elementary school and failed his first college entrance exam. To this day he is considered one of the smartest men that ever lived.
- Clint Eastwood was once told by a University Pictures executive that his future as an actor was not promising. The man said, "You have a chip on your tooth, your Adam's apple sticks out too far, and you talk too slow."

The excuses we make for ourselves on why we can't fulfill our calling could be a book in itself. There are very few of us, if any, that don't have plenty of excuses of why we can't fulfill the will of God. If you look at the path of most successful people, you will find it littered with failure.

Discovering, Developing and Expanding the Real You

The successful don't usually just have more triumphs than most; they also have more falls, since the path to victory is almost always paved with failure. What also sets them apart is their propensity to keep trying and trying.

Babe Ruth is famous for his past home run record, but for decades, he also held the record for strikeouts. He hit 714 home runs and struck out 1,330 times in his career. His attitude was summed up in his own words, "every strike brings me closer to the next home run." Just think about this statement. Thomas Edison tried over 200 different elements before he figured out the right element to use in the light bulb.

Success is a path, a journey, not a destination. In some sense, the definition of any path is what "paves" it. So, while a particular failure may look the same when viewed as a stone on the path, after being placed in context of many stones, it can become the pavement we walk on.

Some of my greatest failures have taught me some of my most meaningful lessons and have built a foundation for what makes me who I am today. If I had not experienced my failures, I would not have the depth of wisdom produced through those adverse circumstances.

We can look at the examples of Moses, Joseph and David to see the concept of this truth, that adversity and failure are many times the foundation for future success. You can see God's hand leading them through adversity and the creative ability of God's Spirit being released in and through their lives.

I think you will find that your greatest work will many times be brought forth in your weakest moment. It is out of the ashes that God brings forth the purest creativity from your life, for He will be the one getting glory. You can't take credit for what is noticeably the hand of God. I have experienced some of my greatest times of creativity when I was going through my darkest hours.

Successful people refuse to allow failure to keep them down. You can't dwell on what might have been and the negative consequences of failure. Learn from mistakes and think about how you can improve yourself and your situation.

FOCUS ON THE THINGS YOU CAN CHANGE

Theodore Roosevelt once said, "Do what you can, with what you have, where you are." If you want to get to where you are going, you have to know where you are going so you can know how to get there. You can't make a map unless you see the world as it is.

Have you ever been to a mall and looked on the map? You see that little red arrow with a dot that says, "You Are Here." To figure out where you are, you are going to have to look at reality. People often look at themselves through the eyes of where they want to be. Vision is great, but to get to your destination, you have to acknowledge where you are at present. It's like putting directions into your GPS. You not only enter the directions to where you are going but also the place where you are starting.

Charles Spurgeon gave us a word of wisdom when he said, "Humility is to make a right estimate of oneself." I have met a number of people who can't see themselves accurately; however, this is a key to moving forward. Paul instructed us to not think more highly of ourselves than we should (Romans 12:3). If we don't accurately assess ourselves, it is impossible to ever fulfill our true potential. To fail in this regard is to live our lives either trying to be someone else or frustrated because we have not met some unrealistic expectation set up by an inflated opinion of ourselves.

The power and pressure to be something other than who you are is something you must continually fight for. We can look at what we consider another person's success and simply emulate what they are doing instead of accurately assessing our own strengths and weaknesses. Just because it works for someone else does not mean you should be doing it, since you can't make yourself something you are not.

Yes, there are things we can change, and it is important to

Discovering, Developing and Expanding the Real You

work on those things. We can change such things as character issues, business procedures, organizational structure, etc., but people often waste enormous amounts of time on things beyond their control.

Growing up, my son was very perceptive about many things. He used to say to me that the person I was gripping at in the car in front of me could not hear me. When we yell at the person going down the road, we are not affecting them because they can't hear us. If I yell at that person, I am not teaching them a lesson and I am not changing the situation. I'm just frustrating myself. Yes, drive away from the person and be safe, but stay focused on what you can change, which is your own personal driving and attitude.

We spend enormous amounts of time and energy trying to make ourselves into something we can never be or trying to change other people into what we want them to be. You can apply this principle to relationships, business interactions, church planting and just about all that you do.

Spending time and effort on situations out of your control is fruitless. To be productive, you must focus on what is in your power to change. You can control your attitudes while on your journey, but you have no control over the actions of others, market forces or even governmental regulations. In using fire as an example: it can be a great benefit if you understand how it works, but it can also burn. You have to understand the type of situation you are dealing with to determine if it is benefiting you or burning you.

The major source of the fear and stress you experience on your journey is many times from things you can do nothing about, so don't focus on those things. Your life will be a lot less stressful when you do what you can do and those things you can't do or that are out of your control you learn to cast those burdens on the Lord.

Discovering, Developing and Expanding the Real You

TURN YOUR FAILURES INTO STEPPING STONES

We can allow our failures to either be burial stones where we let our dreams die or stepping-stones along our journey. When you fail, you need to think about why you failed instead of beating yourself up or blaming someone else for your failure. Turn it into a learning experience. Here are a few questions we can ask ourselves:

- What did I learn from this experience?
- If I were to do it again, what would I do differently?
- Now that this has happened, where do I go from here?
- Was this a failure or an unrealistic dream?
- Where did I succeed as well as fail?

If you sit around pointing fingers at others for your failures, you will never fulfill your purpose. To fulfill your calling, you must continually improve yourself, and you can't do that unless you are willing to take responsibility.

I remember a time when I went through a ministerial train wreck. I was misled and promised things I realized weren't going to happen and I had just moved my entire family 3,000 miles away. Instead of getting mad and demanding what I knew was not going to happen, I decided to act. I did not go out and look for another ministerial position. I found work with a health insurance company and continued working for them while finishing my Bachelor of Science Degree in Business Management.

I took control of my situation. Instead of getting bitter, I chose to make positive steps and through it, I prepared for my future. I am where I am today because I decided to learn from my failure and take proactive action instead of going in circles. You notice I said, "my failure." I failed to judge the situation accurately.

You must develop the ability to learn from your mistakes. Dr. Ronald Niednagel says that, "Failure isn't failure unless you don't learn from it." Two main things we must always remember are to

Discovering, Developing and Expanding the Real You

never stop at failure and to **learn from failure**; these two are inseparable from one another.

THE FRUIT OF HUMILITY IS PERSEVERANCE

Humility is not a quality that comes cheaply. I can't say that I have mastered the quality, but I can say that I have made progress. In my younger years, like most of us, I thought I had most things figured out. It was through actual hands-on experience that I discovered I did not quite have all the answers I thought I did. We must humble ourselves by listening to reality or let denial keep us on the sidelines.

Humility is the personal quality of being free from arrogance and pride. It has an accurate estimate of one's worth. Humility possesses two main aspects. Firstly, it is understanding our complete reliance on the grace of God and secondly, it is living by that grace in conjunction with the gifts we have been given.

We learn reliance on our Father by being a praying person. Prayer is the key to walking in humility and fulfilling the will of God. We can do everything right, but in the end, unless He builds the house, we labor in vain. Jesus, who is our pattern, displayed a life completely reliant on His Father. Jesus depended on Him for everything and if we truly want to fulfill the will of God, we must be dedicated to communion with the Father. Our devotional life before the Lord is the key to developing the perseverance we need to press on to the finish line.

No matter what we have been called to do, if we truly want to complete our mission, we must first be dependent in prayer. John Wesley, the father of the Methodist Church and 17th century revivalist, once said, "I have so much to do that I spend several hours in prayer before I am able to do it."

It is by going through difficulties that we really learn true humility. Every enterprise is going to have to navigate the proverbial icebergs. You can be like the Titanic and go full steam ahead, but you may also suffer the same fate. An aspect of

Discovering, Developing and Expanding the Real You

humility is having the grace to throw in the towel when it is a lost cause. At times it is better to write off a totaled car than to repair it. Starting over or changing paths is sometimes the only way to proceed. It takes wisdom to know the difference between troubled waters and a wrecked ship beyond repair.

Humility slows down; it listens and pays close attention to both outward circumstances and the inward small, still voice of the Spirit. The heart filled with humility does not have all the answers but is willing to listen. The wisdom that comes from the Spirit is pure, peaceable, gentle, reasonable, full of mercy and good fruits, and unwavering, without hypocrisy (James 3:17). Wisdom is humility on display.

I have found that perseverance is the fruit of humility. Humility of heart stays with what God has said and perseveres. If you have listened to the Spirit of God and the wisdom of sound counsel to proceed, then don't give up. When we give up, it is a form of pride combined with unbelief. We must keep our hearts steadfast on the promises of God if we truly want to walk in humility. When we do this, we are agreeing with the grace of God in our lives and the grace He wants to release through our lives.

YOU HAVE A HELPER WHO WILL SEE YOU THROUGH

Although I have felt like throwing in the towel on more than one occasion, the reality of knowing that I am not walking this journey alone has kept me in the race. Romans Chapter 8 has been one of those chapters in the Bible that has kept me going more than once.

During a really difficult time in my life, I felt like I was never going to see the promises of God come to pass. One night in prayer, God brought my attention directly to Romans 8:28, a verse with which you are most likely familiar. It says, "We know that God causes all things to work together for good to those who love God, to those who are called according to His purpose." If you notice, it does not say all things work together for good to everyone. My attention was brought to the words, *"to those who love God.*"

The Greek word for love in this text is *agapaō* and *indicates a direction of the will and finding one's joy in anything.* The text says all is going to work out for our good as long as we direct our will in God's purpose for our lives. It is not the French idea of "Que sera sera" interpreted, as "what will be will be." It's not the idea of the stars aligning and we somehow magically have everything worked out. We just must look around to realize this is not reality.

We must understand that we are in a partnership, and the Spirit of God is hovering over the purpose of the Father in our lives. He is intent on seeing the kingdom of God fully manifested in our lives, but we must set our hearts from start to finish completely on that reality and refuse to settle for anything less.

Paul and Silas just received an open vision about God's open door for them to reach the region of Macedonia (Acts 16:10). In responding in faith to that direction, they found themselves in a prison. Did they say, "Well, I guess we missed God?" No, they joined in with the Holy Spirit and began to praise God, who helped them to fulfill their purpose in the midst of tribulation.

If we want to see the purpose of God fully manifest in our lives, we have to stay in partnership with the Spirit of God. This is the message of Romans 8, and we find this same theme of partnership in John's writings. John refers to the Holy Spirit as the comforter and our advocate, which is unique to his writings. The word *comforter* is a Greek word *parakletos* and is found five times in the New Testament (John 14:16, 26; 15:26; 16:7; I John 2:1). The Vines Expository Dictionary defines this word in the following way: *Called to one's side, to one's aid...it suggests the capability or adaptability of giving aid.*

Learning to live a life of dependence on the Spirit is the only way we will see all things work together for our good. We must learn to press through the pressures we all face on our journey, and it is the Holy Spirit that will give us that strength. God does not take us out of tribulation and pressure, but He actual forms us

Discovering, Developing and Expanding the Real You

in the midst of them if we will allow the fire to fashion the vessel He wants to form.

Viktor Frankl was a Holocaust survivor. He saw death, torture, disease and hopelessness on a daily basis while in the Auschwitz concentration camp. He observed that prisoners who had lost faith in the future, their future, were doomed. With this loss of belief in the future, they also lost their spiritual hold; they let themselves decline and became subject to mental and physical decay.

In a short span of time between Christmas, 1944, and the New Year of 1945, the death rate in Frankl's camp increased beyond all possible expectations, and this is against the background of no visible deterioration of either working or living conditions in the camp. It was simply that the majority of the prisoners had lived in the naive hope they would be home again by Christmas. As the time drew near and there was no encouraging news, the prisoners lost courage and disappointment overcame them. Because this had a dangerous influence on their powers of resistance, a great number of them died.

We cannot allow the troubles of this life to rob us of our dreams. It was Viktor who said, "everything can be taken from a man or a woman but one thing: the last of human freedoms to choose one's attitude in any given set of circumstances, to choose one's own way." As stated at the start of this chapter, we must through much tribulation enter the kingdom of God. The "must" means it is necessary. When do you get to know God and His strength? It is in the tough places of humiliation and brokenness. It is in those places that the Spirit of God is beside you giving you aid.

Settle in your mind that what God has started in you is going to come to pass. You have the choice to keep pressing on or to throw in the towel. When you come to that place, and many times you will, I encourage you to spend time alone with God so the Holy Spirit can encourage you, wash over you and strengthen you to the fulfilling of your dreams.

Discovering, Developing and Expanding the Real You

Appendix 1: Personal Mission Statement

A personal mission statement is what you put into it. Use a pencil since a successful one should always be open to changes as you change, learn and grow. Drawing from it as you continue to pursue your goals in life will help guide you in the positive direction you want your life to go in fulfilling your vision.

I am going to use my personal mission statements as examples. Each should be a two to four sentence statement, which is to the point, clear and concise:

1. **Family**:
   Ex: Develop intimate relationships by setting aside a minimum of 30 minutes per day to spend with my wife and son. Intentionally plan special times with them both.

   _____

   _____

   _____

   _____

2. **Professional Development**:
   Ex: Write books, training material and blogs that are foundational to people's spiritual and practical lives.

   _____

   _____

_____

_____

3. **Finances:**
   Ex: Live debt free and keep our expenses to a minimum. Save for a secure future while giving to help those in need.

   _____

   _____

   _____

   _____

4. **Physical** (exercise and eating):
   Ex: Maintain a healthy body that can be used to its fullest potential. Run 15 miles per week. Eat nutritional food that is low in sodium. Get a yearly medical physical.

   _____

   _____

   _____

   _____

Discovering, Developing and Expanding the Real You

5. **Social**:
   Ex.: Spend time with other believers at a minimum twice a week in an open sharing community. Invite friends over to our house; be involved with a running club or community organization.

   _____

   _____

   _____

   _____

6. **Spiritual Development**:
   Ex.: Grow in faith daily, learning how to be a mature son of my Father. Spend at a minimum one-hour daily in prayer, study and meditation.

   _____

   _____

   _____

   _____

Appendix 2: Lists and Checklist

I am giving you a personal example of how I have used a list and checklist in helping me fulfill my personal goals and mission statement. You can use this for homeschooling, running a business or any endeavor, you are undertaking. The example list and checklist are over a one-week period of time.

List - Things To Do

	Family
1.	Read marriage book.
2.	30 minutes going over schoolwork with son.
3.	Eat dinner nightly.
4.	Prayer time w/family.
5.	Talk over the day with my wife.

	Professional
1.	Read 'Talent Is Never Enough" by John Maxwell.
2.	Write 1 hour nightly.
3.	Interact on Facebook and Twitter

Checklist – Things Done

Family
Read marriage book 4 days and finished 30 pages
Went over schoolwork w/son every day and ran with him.
Ate dinner 3 nights and prayed 5 nights.
Talked nightly with wife.

Professional
Read 20 pages of 'Talent'
Wrote a new blog post.
Worked 6 hours on book *Start To Finish*.
Spent 1 hour every night interacting on FB/Twitter.

Discovering, Developing and Expanding the Real You

	Finances
1.	Meet our weekly food budget.
2.	Don't drive more than necessary.
3.	Communicate with my wife about our needs, wants and savings.

	Finances
	Cooked a crockpot of chicken for the week.
	Communicated with my wife to get needed items each trip to town.

	Physical
1.	Eat a healthy breakfast and lunch.
2.	Run three miles daily.
3.	Stretch every day before bed.

	Physical
	I ate boiled eggs and fruit for breakfast.
	Ate a large lunch and small dinner.
	Ran 10 miles and walked 8.
	Stretched 3 nights.

	Social
1.	Run with running club once a week.
2.	Attend one or two church meetings weekly.

	Social
	Had breakfast with a local pastor.
	Fellowshipped Sunday morning with the church.
	Had a couple over to the house after service.

	Spiritual
1.	Spend one hour nightly in prayer and bible study.

	Spiritual
	Prayed and studied for 2 hours nightly.

Discovering, Developing and Expanding the Real You

If it will help you; then cut out the next two pages and make copies. Use this as a template for any goals you are trying to accomplish.

List - Things To Do

Checklist – Things Done

Discovering, Developing and Expanding the Real You

List - Things To Do   ## Checklist – Things Done

Discovering, Developing and Expanding the Real You

---

[1] "Roaring Lambs", by Bob Briner, Zondervan 1993, Pg. 47-48.

[2] "Leadership, Management and The Five Essentials for Success", Pg. 10-11 by Rick Joyner, MorningStar Publications 1990.

[3] "Leadership, Management and The Five Essentials for Success", Pg. 149 by Rick Joyner MorningStar Publications 1990.

[4] "Linchpin" by Seth Godin, Pg. 183, Penguin Group 2010

[5] "The Starfish and The Spider" by Ori Brafman and Rod A. Beckstrom, Pg. 200.

[6] "On The Verge", by Alan Hirsch and Dave Ferguson, Zondervan: Grand Rapids, Michigan 2011 Pg. 56.

[7] "Rosa Parks" by Douglas Brinkley, New York: Lipper-Viking. 2000

[8] "On The Verge", by Alan Hirsch and Dave Ferguson, Zondervan: Grand Rapids, Michigan 2011 Pg. 32.

[9] "Catholic Bible Dictionary", by Scott Hahn, Doubleday 2009, Pg. 255.

[10] "Shift" by Peter Arnell, Broadway Books 2010, Pg. 29.

[11] "Launch: How To Quickly Propel Your Business Beyond Your Competitors", Michael Stelzner, Pg. 8,10.

Discovering, Developing and Expanding the Real You

---

[12] "Permanent Revolution" by Alan Hirsch and Tim Catchim, Josey-Bass 2012, Pg. 186.

[13] "Linchpin" by Seth Godin, Penguin Group 2010, Pg. 180.

[14] "Organic Leadership" by Neil Cole, Baker Books, 2009 Pg. 141-142.

[15] "Permanent Revolution" by Alan Hirsch and Tim Catchim, Josey-Bass 2012, Pg. 8

[16] "Permanent Revolution" by Alan Hirsch and Tim Catchim, Josey-Bass 2012, Pg. 29.